e-Leadership

GUIDING

YOUR BUSINESS

TO SUCCESS IN

THE NEW ECONOMY

D. QUINN MILLS, Ph.D.

Prentice
Hall Press

Library of Congress Cataloging-in-Publication Data

Mills, Daniel Quinn.
   E-leadership : guiding your business to success / D. Quinn Mills.
      p.   cm.
   Includes index.
   ISBN 0-7352-0225-7
    1. Leadership.   2. Industrial management—Data processing.   3. Internet.
  I. Title.

   HD57.7.M543 2001
   658.4'092—dc21

                                   00-064989

Printed in the United States of America

10 9 8 7 6 5 4 3 2 1

ISBN 0-7352-0225-7

ATTENTION: CORPORATIONS AND SCHOOLS

Prentice Hall Press books are available at quantity discounts with bulk purchase for educational, business, or sales promotional use. For information, please write to: Prentice Hall Press Special Sales, 240 Frisch Court, Paramus, New Jersey 07652. Please supply: title of book, ISBN, quantity, how the book will be used, date needed.

Products and company names herein may be the trademarks or registered trademarks of their respective owners.

 Paramus, NJ 07652

http://www.phdirect.com

acknowledgments

THE AUTHOR WISHES TO THANK MR. IAIN SOMERVILLE AND Mr. G. Bruce Friesen of Andersen Consulting for their assistance in the thinking and research that led to this book, and the Harvard Business School for financial support of the research and preparation of the book.

introduction

THE E-LEADER GUIDES A NONTRADITIONAL FIRM TO SUCCESS in the new economy. He or she may be expert in the new technology, but that isn't absolutely required. What is required is to identify those who are and support them, even stepping out of their way if necessary—to let newer people point the direction of the company or to recognize who among longer-service employees have an affinity for the new and give them initiative—and to build an organizational framework (positions and culture) in which the new can displace the old. This is the core of e-Leadership. It's what this book is about.

Three questions should continually occupy the e-Leader, whatever the size of his or her firm:

- **How are new technologies creating opportunities that would let me build a bigger, better business?**

- Where is new technology creating pitfalls that could sink my firm?

- How do I manage the increasing complexity of teamwork among ambitious specialists working in my organization and those who are in other organizations but work with my people?

This book answers these questions with a new approach for those who are going to be e-Leaders—people who can help a firm navigate through the stormy seas that new technology creates to gain the prizes it offers. E-Leaders depend on experience with the Internet because technological change is one of today's most important sources of the unexpected. To reflect the lessons of the Internet this book proposes that successful e-Leaders focus on two things:

1. a new approach to market development

2. a new approach to implementing strategy

But technology alone isn't enough of a base for today's new leaders; the other, related source of relevant experience is the global economy. To accommodate it, I propose:

1. a new organizational structure: a form of network termed a global lattice; and

2. a new corporate culture, namely, the global mindset.

A firm that adopts these is physically and "mentally" prepared to take advantage of global opportunities and resources, and protected against being blindsided by competitors.

In the following pages are key insights into twenty-first–century business. This book is based on, but is not a detailed presentation of, extensive research; it presents, but does not insist upon, a distinct point of view. Its purpose is to present new ideas, concepts, and approaches that you can adopt in whole or in part as suits your circumstances. This, in my experience, is the greatest value many busy executives derive from research studies—a few key ideas that they can employ to improve their companies' sales, productivity, and profitability.

Traditional thinking about strategy, organization, and leadership is missing from this book; instead, it presents new ideas about each. It goes beyond traditional thinking about organization, for example, to applying resources from a variety of firms against opportunities; beyond the notion of employee satisfaction to that of energizing a company; beyond identifying a firm's competencies to emphasizing a firm's potential; beyond conventional strategy-making to a new three-step process for decentralized planning; and beyond global operations to global value creation.

There are four doors into twenty-first–century business, one each for market development, organization, culture, and strategic implementation. This book opens each and finds behind the door for business development, the business array; behind the door for organization, the lattice; behind the door for culture, a global mindset; and behind the door for strategy implementation, a three-step process that brings speed to planning and planning to all levels of the organization.

In too much of today's business, writing insights cannot be applied because they are taken to logical extremes. In effect, executives are offered ornaments without a tree. This book is about the tree. It presents a comprehensive view of a company focusing on a new way of creating value in the global economy.

contents

Part III. Powering via a Global Mindset

Part IV. Speeding Through Decentralized Planning

Part V. Leading for Opportunity

Part VI. Making Arrays, Mindset, and Speed Work for You

how e-leaders realize full value for their companies

the e-Leader recognizes that leadership is outdated today unless it helps people deal with the great challenges offered by technological innovations and the emergence of the new economy. His or her mission is to develop new approaches by which people are better able to recognize, understand, and master the new world.

Times of transition sometimes turn accepted approaches on their heads and render them counterproductive. This is very hard for people to accept, and increases the pressure on executives to provide leadership. For example, the most basic principle of business strategy is that strategy must drive structure—that is, that a company should first determine its strategy, then design its organization to carry out the strategy. This is usually a sound and logical proposition, but not always. Following it too closely in today's world of the Internet may ruin a firm. Instead, it's better to turn the formula upside down, to reorganize, and then to work out the company's strategy.

There are two reasons for this surprising proposition:

1. **Unless leaders have the right organization and people, they and their planners won't have access to information about key opportunities in the new age, so that the strategy process will be blind.**

2. **The right organization staffed with ambitious, impatient people will require of the leader a strategy that will keep them with the firm, and so preserve it from traditional, overly cautious planning.**

For both reasons getting the organization right precedes making strategy; the world is topsy-turvy.

But where are the leaders to bring such a change to their companies? They've not been trained in schools or corporate training programs, because this is too new. They've had to learn it through hard experience. The rest of us can learn from them what it means to be an e-Leader.

Today, for a few years, structure is going to drive strategy: The right structure will help you identify opportunities, and it will put on the pressure to develop an effective strategy. Without the right structure, strategy is going to be unimaginative and timid. (Structure and what it is will be described later in Chapter 3.)

More surprising results of the technological changes that are creating our new economy are recounted in the following pages. In academia, each new proposition causes bitter controversy. This book will not attempt to prove each to the satisfaction of academics—there are other forums in which to pursue that objective. In these pages our purpose is to give executives and managers new ideas that are likely to prove helpful in their businesses.

How to create significant value in today's increasingly interconnected world economy is our core concern. The story told here is about how people, limited by misconceptions based on past experience, make errors in the new business environment. It is also about helping executives get beyond these misconceptions by opening their eyes to new vistas:

- so much unrealized potential that even market leaders are falling short
- so much opportunity that what matters most is potential—competencies your company doesn't yet have; markets it doesn't yet serve

what is the role of the e-leader?

Broadly, it's the role of the e-Leader to succeed in the new economy. This, however, is too general a proposition. In this book I suggest that it is going to take a certain number of steps:

1. To help older employees be managed and led by people younger in age but more experienced in the new economy;

2. To open the culture of a long-existing firm to unfettered communication, and to keep the open culture of a start-up, despite the need for structure in the organization;

3. To get ownership in the company to everyone, just as start-ups now give stock options to every employee;

4. To build and keep an environment in which it is exciting to work—not one in which employees are merely satisfied (this is the old model);

5. To link the company to others that can help it build its products and markets, not just by contracts and transactions, but more important by a nurturing flow of information and ideas; and

6. To develop managers who can pursue a strategic direction despite continual changes in market conditions without having continually to seek guidance from above, and be paralyzed while waiting for it to come.

Specific ways to do each of these things are presented in the following chapters—specific directions for becoming an e-Leader.

CHAPTER 1

the unrealized potential

OUR INCREASINGLY NETWORKED WORLD IS ALIVE WITH opportunities that even today's market leaders are unable to fully exploit. Day by day the potential increases as information technology entices a world drawn ever closer with opportunities for electronic commerce. Today's top firms report record earnings and share price peaks, but their chief executives know that the full potential of the networked economy continues to elude them. Growth is difficult, if rates of return are compared to the cost of invested capital. Many firms that appear profitable are not returning their cost of capital.

To create more value, e-Leaders need something new and radical that traditional concepts of strategy and organization don't provide.

Even as firms cope with a changing world by doing things differently, many people don't really understand why they are being forced to change. If they did, they could more fully exploit the attendant value-creation potential.

This book introduces four key concepts for business: the business array; the organizational lattice; the global mindset; and strategic speed. It shows how to turn the strategic concept of an array into the practical reality of an array-map, and how to proceed to select activities and define the optimal role for a company. It also describes how to build and manage the lattice organization structure that gives shape to the resources contributed by companies to a market opportunity. It shows how global mindset powers the culture of a firm. Last, it shows how strategic speed can be attained by a lattice. This final element is crucial because a lattice consists of elements of various firms—and if each firm pursues a traditional lengthy planning-to-execution process, the lattice will be too slow to act to be successful in today's marketplace.

Thus the four elements discussed—which may seem to be separate and unrelated—are in fact crucial to business success in the wired world and therefore to each other. The array is the setting in which opportunities are identified; the lattice is the device by which they are pursued; the global mindset is the key to a culture that seizes opportunities; and strategic speed is the process by which a marketplace advantage over competitors is obtained.

profiting from business arrays

An array can best be described as the marketplace neighborhood of a firm—the locale in which it gets its brand established, implements any standards that it can make proprietary, and determines its relationships with its customers.

Value is created by leveraging a firm's position in a business array: a group of enterprises, organizations, and individuals that in working for themselves also work toward a common objective. Firms in an array may have formal relationships (for example, buyer and supplier, joint venture, alliance) or simply be moving in the same direction. An array is, however, broader than particular relationships and less formal. It might include, for example, firms that have explicit alliances with each other, but is not necessarily disrupted when alliances end. By formal and informal relationships within an array, a firm brings itself to the attention of potential customers and obtains the opportunity to build its own relationships with them.

Arrays exist in all areas of the world economy and business executives are aware of them and act to influence them, but they've received far less analysis than they deserve. Arrays have come to the fore in the thinking of many executives because of their centrality in Internet space.

In Internet space a company has three major problems:

1. **How to get noticed—to get its brand recognized**

2. **How to attract, motivate, and retain talent for whom there is enormous demand**

3. **How to move fast enough to get ahead and stay ahead of the competition**

The methods are, in simplest formulation: to get attention, be effective, and be fast. But how?

Consider, for example, an Internet start-up that offers working adults the opportunity to take college courses on-line.

Colleges (for example, Syracuse University, Bellevue College, and Penn State) have been active in putting courses on the Internet. Firms such as Sylvan Learning, Convene, Real Education, and Blackboard sell to colleges the technology needed to make college courses available via the Internet. Other firms provide detailed information about colleges (such as collegetown.usa and petersons.com), and commercial firms located near them offer books for college courses (for example, cyberclassics.com), catalogue adult education courses for each metropolitan area (as in takeaclass.com), and help to create the market for higher education by profiling job opportunities for people with particular skills and credentials (such as Monster.com, which lists job opportunities).

All of these firms are in one way or another promoting Internet-delivered higher education; each expects to profit from doing so. They support the broad endeavor of providing a ubiquitous alternative to campus-based college education in different ways: the InternetU.com by focusing on marketing college courses; Bellevue College by providing courses over the Internet; Sylvan, Convene, Real Education, WebCT, and Blackboard by focusing on technology used to bring college courses to the Internet; Cyberclassics by focusing on book sales; and Monster by focusing on job placement.

Each of these firms and institutions is trying to bring itself to the attention of customers. None of these firms knows for sure where the bulk of the value created by Internet-delivered education will be captured, whether in marketing, technology, book sales, course content, or jobs. But each works in parallel with the others while trying to maximize its share of the value. To develop such a market sufficiently to be financially successful would be prohibitively expensive for a single firm; a business array effectively shares the costs of market development.

We have described an array in Internet space. Arrays also exist outside of Internet space in some of our oldest industries. Las Vegas firms compete vigorously for visitors by building great casinos and hotels, for example, because they know that the number of visitors grows as the strip becomes larger and more exciting, so they physically link their properties. The strip is a product of an array that includes not only competitors, but also suppliers, as well as firms concerned with neither that exist to serve the multitudes that are drawn to Las Vegas. This array—of cooperating and competing firms and the firms that in some way support them—is evident to the most casual observer.

Another example of a business array from physical space is the explosion of high-end food markets on the west side of Manhattan. Since 1975 the number of markets has tripled, fueling both customer interest and fierce competition among several of the shops.[1] Yet for most of these firms, the other firms in the geographic area and serving the same or similar customers are not so much competitors as allies in building consumer recognition of the general product line and geographic area in which to shop. All shops benefit from this market building. For a single shop, other companies—even if not full allies, and still competitors to a degree—are at best quasi-competitors.

The strategic issue presented to a firm by the array in which it exists is to choose and establish a desired relationship with quasi-competitors.

Inasmuch as it involves directing resources against an opportunity or portfolio of opportunities, a business array can cross firm, industry, national, and political lines. It has an information flow so is like a network, a structure so its organization can be analyzed—but it is not a form of business organization; rather it's a grouping of firms just as is an industry. All of these characteristics are manifested in a virtual value space, and therein lies the true potential of an array.

How is a business array distinguished from a value-chain? An array is a different concept. In Las Vegas, for example, the hotels—interconnecting and differentiating—build a market from which they all benefit. Is this a value-chain? No, the value-chain is larger (it includes more upstream elements) and narrower (there's a value-chain for each hotel, and the other hotels don't enter it).

An array is a concept crucial to market development. The array is a particular stage (or point) in a value-chain; it's smaller than an industry, but larger than an individual firm. For most purposes an array has a geographic dimension, but in Internet space it is immediately global (though currently restricted to a degree by the reach of national languages).

Traditionally we think of many of the members of an array as a company's competitors, but in fact (as the Las Vegas and Internet examples show) there may be as much synergy as competition. Understanding this is crucial to building the proper alliances, reaching customers, and so on, where firms have limited resources. Marketing and branding on the Internet are created through business development (that is, relations with other firms) and the array clarifies our thinking in how to do this.

In today's world, an e-Leader seeks optimal market positioning by placing the firm in an array in such a way as to capture a disproportionate amount of the value that is being created. Microsoft's exploitation a decade ago of a business array in an emerging industry is illustrative, allowing it to seize dominance of the personal computer market.

In choosing an arena of opportunity—the emerging microcomputer (as it was then called) market—Bill Gates and Paul Allen joined an array of firms acting in concert to try to create value from the product. It was not obvious that they would be able to do so. Xerox, although it had developed a prototype in its Palo Alto labs, had not brought the microcomputer to market, in large part, according to former chief executive David Kearns, because the company had not been able to persuade itself that the product could be profitable.

Apple was a start-up which didn't ask that question, electing to pursue instead a vision of taking computers out of the glass houses and giving them to individuals. When dominant player IBM entered, it called its product by a name that would come to be applied to the industry generally, the personal computer or PC.

A number of arrays were created around the personal computer. One centered on Apple, another on IBM.

Microsoft positioned itself with other firms, including Intel, in the IBM array.

Initially an insignificant participant, Microsoft developed an understanding of value creation involving personal computers. Gates and Allen believed the customer's perception of value to be changing in such a way that the operating system would occupy a key position in the array. They were right; much of the utility of personal computers turned out to be tied (even before the Internet) to communications between computers, making the operating system central to value creation because it was by sharing a common operating system—at that time—that people could communicate among computers.

In the years-long process by which it seized the central position of value-creation in its array, Microsoft pursued its vision and when the operating system emerged at the center of the value of the PC to customers, the company was in a position to secure a disproportionate share of the value created by the array as a whole. In its final step, Microsoft sought to secure the value made possible by its positioning. A key incident occurred when the firm delayed the introduction of the new Windows operating system in order to derive a longer value contribution from its previous system: DOS. In a final step, Microsoft separated the personal computer from the large computer array. Although it remained a leader in the latter, IBM was relegated to a lesser participant in the PC array, in which Microsoft became the dominant player. This separation of the PC from the computer generally caused observers to distinguish between a supposed PC and a large computer industry, although both were in reality part of the same industry and what had really been separated were arrays.

designing an organizational lattice

How should a firm be configured so as to seize opportunities created by new business arrays? This is a key issue for the e-Leader because building an effective organization is the key to turning opportunity into reality.

The conventional answer today to how to organize a firm is the network organization; but it's too informal to be effective. What is required is an extension of today's network, a lattice composed of connected elements that share a formal structure, but still provides for extensive customization to meet specific applications. A step beyond the network organization, the lattice imposes order on what have been loose protocols.

The lattice is the means by which a firm exploits the potential in a business array. The array is a concept in strategy with organizational implications. That is to say, the business array is a concept in strategy analysis; the lattice, a concept in organization design. Both are new and both are important.

A lattice is owned by no single entity but creates value for all. It has only minimal formal structure, but is not chaotic. It derives regularity and predictability from:

- **a common infrastructure for information management and knowledge exchange**
- **a common commitment to build value in a specific area**

- strict use of logic of market forces (each unit within the lattice performs well-defined tasks and has distinct buyers)

A lattice is much more flexible than other forms of organization. All organizations (big and small) have formal hierarchies (with empowerment or without). A lattice, however, can operate without a formal hierarchy (that is, without formal authority of one unit over another; or it can be given a formal hierarchy and authority).

The lattice is made up of elements from several different firms. Thereby, it allows more risk than one organization could accept. This is important because in developing new products and services there is much more risk than in simply extending an existing set of market offerings; but there is also much more potential value to be created. The essence of the valuation-creation opportunities lies in market innovation and that is risky; so firms seek arrangements by which that risk can be shared. The business array is an informal method of spreading risk: Firms work together in the same direction. The lattice is a more formal, organizational method: Firms link themselves in a flexible structure to pursue a business opportunity while spreading the risk among themselves.

Flexibility and the capability to reconfigure assets, people, and activities are essential for survival and growth in today's unstable environment.

The lattice also leverages the specialized intellectual capability of different firms. That is, because of lattices a firm need not possess all the specialized capability a particular business initiative may require.

A lattice is a mixture of matrix management, outsourcing, and the virtual organization. A lattice is complex in management structure like a matrix. Because it includes elements from different firms, it is a bit like outsourcing from the perspective of any single firm. Finally, the lattice relies on modern electronic communication technology to facilitate teamwork creating—virtual organizations.

A lattice may be thought of as a device for focusing human energy on a business opportunity. This device must contain people bringing required skills to bear on the opportunity; extraneous resources or unnecessary capabilities are luxuries detracting from value creation. These resources and capabilities must be given a means of coherent action; this is done by defining business processes, sequences of activities that, when performed, generate value. Thus, a lattice is a device that aligns people around business processes to deliver value.

Lattices are important because this is how strategy and execution are carried out on a global basis in a networked world. The unique contribution of the notion of a lattice is to identify the grouping of organizational elements necessary to act effectively.

Businesses now employ, in various combinations and numerous variations, five major forms of organization: hierarchy, matrix, cluster, network, and lattice. The most recent, the lattice, is only now being employed and analyzed. It is emerging to meet the new challenges of today's business environment. Its significance lies less in its structure than in its central concern. Structure, it is said, should follow strategy, and this is so; but structure must also conform to context by eschewing traditional organizational forms that seem tied to strategic directions, but which in fact are outdated means to attain strategic goals.

The central concern of a network is influence and support (for example, "Who can I get to help me with this or that?"), a concept so undefined and lacking in structure as to lose much usefulness when applied in a firm. Network is a broad category that often means little more than an individual's web of acquaintances.

The lattice is a network with structure that imparts a different central concern: the relationship of parts to one another and to the whole. The central concern of a lattice is neither control nor delegation, but rather arranging organizational elements so as to foster synergy through cooperation. Because a lattice often involves individuals or units not in the same firm, the sort of control exercised in a hierarchy or matrix is not possible. For example, a business development team in a large company might draw members from suppliers and alliance firms, but cannot manage them so directly as it does its own people.

There are many different applications of the general form (or ideal type) of lattice. But all share the objective of developing cooperative relations among the parts to generate value-creating synergy around a business opportunity.

The lattice is designed to resolve the paradoxes that bedevil modern business: the desire to be both global and local, to both control and empower employees, to be both the best and also the least costly. To resolve such conundrums, the lattice avoids traditional strategy. Because there is no analytic solution, no algorithm, it pursues solutions via repeated computations, not by formula, but by working through trial after trial in much the same way simultaneous equations are solved. There is, in effect, no structural or strategic solution, only an executional solution. The point is to avoid being forced by analysis to make undesirable tradeoffs.

A lattice is much more flexible than other forms of organization. Its unique contribution is to identify effective, value-creating groupings of organizational and extra-organizational elements.

moving quickly

Electronic connectivity, market deregulation, and advanced technologies of many sorts are obliterating structural barriers to competition. Quick and effective response to change are often all that protect a company's position. General Motor's Saturn Division, for example, quickly developed brand identification with a small car, but when the oil crisis ended, General Motors was not prepared to make the additional investments necessary to reposition the brand and lost most of the market momentum Saturn had built. In Internet space, Netscape sacrificed to Microsoft and other competitors the dominant position it held by failing to move quickly enough to enhance its offerings, by failing to acquire Vermeer's Front Page; while Microsoft was actively seeking to purchase Vermeer. (Netscape phoned to invite Vermeer's principals to give Netscape a call if they were interested in selling the firm.)

Microsoft has achieved unprecedented speed to market by means of a device that frightens most executives. It introduces products before they are fully debugged, relying on customers to identify and report shortcomings to the company. Being first to market has often caused potential competitors to shy away. Although many customers avoid early versions of Microsoft products, expecting imperfections, being first to market is sufficiently advantageous to Microsoft to offset the loss of early customers.

Firms that lack Microsoft's dominant position tend to be reluctant to introduce imperfect products. Speed, however, remains essential. What is needed is a disciplined process for making products of high quality very quickly. To achieve speed a firm must first abandon the archaic separation of strategy and execution, and planning and implementation. These must be much more closely linked, intertwined around one another in time in the manner of a double helix.

Firms must do more—faster. They must decentralize strategic planning to the business unit level, and do so in such a way that it can be successfully and speedily accomplished by business unit managers without significant staff or resources for consulting. In effect, business unit managers need to become more like entrepreneurs in their own markets.

The route to continuous decentralized planning follows a three-step process of seeking, shaping, and securing. In general, seeking is about discovering opportunity, shaping is about locking in the opportunity, and securing is about seizing value.

This three-step process calls for business units to continually assess their marketplace situation, and seek and exploit opportunities as they emerge. Many opportunities are likely to be missed by a centralized strategic planning process because of slow action and inadequate knowledge. Moreover, division-level managers ordinarily lack both strategic planning skills and the financial resources for extensive consulting help. Overcoming these impediments is accomplished by supplementing the budget process—with the three intuitive steps of seeking, shaping, and securing. With continuous decentralized planning, top executives can check business unit planning by posing questions about targets, methods, and results of business initiatives.

The advantages of strategic speed are threefold:

1. It enables a firm to operate on a global stage, moving products, capital, and labor from where they are cheap to where they are dear.

2. It enables a firm to exploit synergy, to integrate concepts drawn from varied sources to create new ideas. A global enterprise finds great value in synergy precisely because it has access to so many divergent sources of ideas and to the knowledge exchange tools that accommodate their blending in new ways. Incredible value is to be found in diversity of perspective, provided it can be successfully integrated.

3. Strategic speed enables a firm to hedge, to construct portfolios of activities with offsetting returns to reduce combined risk. Portfolio theory from finance suggests that blending investments with variable returns—provided the variances are negatively correlated—can yield fixed returns. Although this notion has lost credibility with the financial crises in hedge

funds, the latter have been due to misuse of the principle. Notwithstanding their name, hedge funds don't hedge; they speculate. Hedging, moreover, can apply to any asset, be it people, factories, or local markets. A global enterprise is positioned to extract great value from hedging by virtue of its geographic dispersion and knowledge-exchange tools. A global enterprise can potentially build stability on a foundation of variability by actively balancing dispersed activities in many markets.

Each of these capabilities is central to success in today's business world, and each is a product of strategic speed.

points to remember

The e-Leader recognizes that the twenty-first century is presenting a new type of opportunity that even today's best firms are not seizing.

- Further technological advances and the electronic networking of the world promise vastly favorable new business economics.

- Unfortunately, most contemporary business organizations are incapable of exploiting what technology and global scope are making possible.

- Building economic value on a large scale in the next century will require leaders to do some very different things, in particular:

  position their firms in business arrays (that is, groups of firms working together to build value);

  build a global lattice as a way to harness resources;

  create a global mindset; and

  adopt continuous decentralized strategic planning in business units.

- Global business success can be achieved by a new three-step approach involving:

  Seeking (searching around the globe and selecting the best opportunities);

  Shaping (setting the stage to apply resources and capabilities); and

  Securing (seizing the value).

These three steps embody the bias to action that must be present in its decentralized and geographically dispersed units for an e-Leader to lead a firm to success in the twenty-first century.

CHAPTER 2

the value-creation
opportunity

big opportunities, difficult context

IN BROAD PERSPECTIVE THE 1990S HAVE BEEN A HEYDAY FOR
many companies. The American economy has had a business
expansion of unprecedented duration. The globalization of
business—the disorderly convergence of separate national
markets into one—has been supported by technological
and geopolitical forces alike, abetted by improvements in
transportation and communication, and the collapse of
communism. This has brought billions of people and vast
regions into the markets served by Western business.

The decade ahead is not likely to be so favorable. The directions of technology and geopolitics will diverge: technology continuing to be supportive of business, geopolitics
less so.

The next few years will be turbulent as forces for global
business collide with countervailing forces, including a

backlash against globalization. Although unlikely to be sus-tained owing to increasing connectivity between coun-tries, this backlash will pose a very real, if short-term, impediment to firms striving to push forward with value creation. The e-Leader will have to master this turbulent environment.

shifting from the old to the new economics

Connectivity is creating a new economics that holds enormous potential for value creation. It has the capacity to drive the cost of acquiring customers close to zero, to impose substantial switching penalties that, in effect, "lock" others into their value chains, and to reduce capital requirements without materially affecting revenues and so sharply increase returns to shareholders and other stakeholders.

The new economics is further enhanced by global reach: the connectivity-supported integration of national and re-gional markets for capital, labor, products, and services. This emerging market "space" is presenting opportunities to re-duce costs and lever assets such as brands in fundamentally new ways. But these opportunities will elude companies that are unable to shed outdated strategic concepts and organiza-tional approaches designed for the old economics.

Industry-based business strategy focused on specific mar-ket niches required certain organizational competencies to support its execution. Superior returns were generated less by seeking new insights through knowledge exchange (which was left to entrepreneurs and academics) than by finding "barriers to entry" such as unique resources, costly physical assets, regulations, or proprietary patents that could keep rivals from initiating the life-cycle supporting process of technology diffusion.

In the old economics, companies sought either to become low-cost providers or to differentiate themselves from rivals to support higher operating costs as they grew in size and scope. The longer competitors could be kept from learning critical secrets or concepts for satisfying a particular market need, the greater the total returns that could be wrung from an innovation before its inevitable demise. The walls and moats with which companies surrounded themselves and their operations took various forms, among them:

- **buying employee loyalty with the concepts of life-long employment career advancement, and rising pay;**

- **maintaining "in-house" functions and departments required to support their business operations; and**

- **tightly controlling (that is hoarding and restricting the dissemination of) information.**

The creation, synthesis, integration, and management ideas allowed by steadily increasing connectivity among persons of diverse perspectives, knowledge, and experience is the principal driver of the new economics. Advances in information technology that have increased bandwidth and storage capacity, and facilitated access to and manipulation of information are the progenitors of the connectivity phenomenon. The advantageous economics of networks can be observed in any professional community of practice. The larger the number of significant contributors in a well-managed firm, the proportionally higher the potential return, hence, rising returns to scale.

If two heads are better than one for solving problems, then more than two heads correctly managed are likely to be even better. The totality of a community's membership has the potential to be much more than the sum of its parts. New members not only increase the sum of a community's knowledge through the addition of their own, but also enhance that body of knowledge through interaction that generates new insights, in a word, through synergy. It is this many-fold association that holds the promise of significant positive returns.

Gains to scale from connectivity are limited only by the pace of physical interconnection and speed with which the interconnecting entities learn how to make connectivity work for them.

The prospect of sustained and even accelerating returns of scale has powerful practical implications for companies.

- **With raw materials, conversion capability, and labor accessible anywhere in the world, the basic costs of doing business can be driven down to the lowest price for the requisite resources.**

- **Strong incentives can be employed to discourage customers from turning to other providers.**

- **Through multipartner alliances, companies virtually devoid of assets beyond their particular knowledge bases can derive nearly infinite returns from coordinating the work of others.**

Even the best companies are failing to realize the full potential of globalization.

- Multinational companies "live in many places, but do not act as if everywhere is their home."

- If "everywhere" was their home, they would not duplicate domestic ways of doing business around the world.

- They would be both local and global in their values, processes, and behaviors.

the three myopias that prevent firms from realizing potential value from globalization

strategic myopia

- The new world is "dynamic/emergent," requiring nonlinear thinking.

- Competitive advantages are executional, not structural (that is, there are few "barriers").

- Globalization demands local and global cost and value optimization.

- Leveraging competencies is not enough; opportunities must be recognized and exploited.

organizational myopia

- The old world was self-contained, functional, hierarchical, centralized.

- The new world is alliance-enabled, process-oriented, networked, distributed.

leadership myopia

- The old world was centralized and directive, premised on the notion of direct reports ("command and control").
- The new world is decentralized, diplomatic, networked ("hyperhierarchical").

In a world that is restructuring economically, executives—like investors—must search globally to find growth. World trade is growing as are direct foreign and international investment. Even if world growth as a whole is relatively slow, opportunities nevertheless abound for business.

If a company has a presence on the Internet, as companies are increasingly likely to do, it is global without necessarily intending to be. But being global does not yield value by default. Globalization is a fertile context for value creation. The new business economics generates opportunities that must be exploited to create value.

The trend in the old economics for returns to additional investments in a business to trail off rapidly after a short period—termed *decreasing returns to scale* by economists—dictates both prices and returns to investors. The opportunity to secure new customers at little or no cost and later impose on them substantial switching costs promises huge potential returns to investors. It constitutes, in effect, a law of increasing returns to scale: the more one invests, the higher not just the return, but the rate of return. Effects of this law can be glimpsed in the enormous success of some Internet-based start-up firms. No wonder top executives of large firms are both dazzled by opportunity and worried that they will not be its beneficiaries, but its victims. For those likely to become victims, adapting to the new world is an issue not only of unrealized potential, but of survival. To benefit rather than be victimized by the new business economics, companies must find new, value-creating ways of doing business.

Even leading high-tech firms are not entirely in step with the new world. Having committed in 1995 to developing the Internet, Microsoft became a major contributor to the connected world. One might expect the company responsible for products that enable virtual teams, virtual organizations, and the virtual corporations to avail itself of the opportunities created thereby. But when it acquired in early 1996 Massachusetts-based Vermeer Technology, Microsoft moved the firm's 38 software developers and their families clear across the continent to Redmond, Washington. Microsoft can take as a tribute to its reputation as a firm that respects engineers, the Vermeer engineers' unilateral acceptance of the pilgrimage; but in uprooting so many people, it revealed itself to be a very traditional firm that forsakes the very opportunities it promotes to those to whom it markets its products.

The challenges of adapting to it notwithstanding, technological advance is good for business. The bad news for business has mostly to do with national governments.

coping with uneven growth

Companies become global to grow. But where is the double-digit growth to which many have made commitments to investors to be found, when the economies of the United States and most other industrialized nations are forecasted to grow at only 2 percent or 3 percent per year over the next decade?

Most Americans believe the world is to be in a period of rapid economic expansion, with less developed nations progressing towards the consumption standards of the developed nations. Some pundits write of a coming 20-year long boom. Unfortunately, the available data doesn't support these scenarios.

Although high in some less developed nations, growth rates are slipping in others.[1] In the world as a whole, as in the United States, the rate of per-capita economic growth is on a long-term decline (see Table 2-1). This is a function not of population growth soaring—in fact, it is falling—but of the engines of growth slowing down.

> **Note:** The growth rate of each country is weighted by its volume of economic activity. The United States, for example, is weighted heavily. If calculations are made using population weights, the overall world growth rate changes very little. Although firm figures are not yet available, preliminary estimates indicate that 2001 will not exceed the average growth rate for the period 1993–2000. If current projections—which show slowdowns in Asia, North America, and much of Europe—are correct, 2001 will fall short of the 1993–2000 rate. The growth

Table 2-1 Worldwide Per-Capita Economic Growth: Average Annual Growth Rates 1960–2000

1960–1980	1980–1992	1993–2000
4.0%	1.9%	1.3%

rate average for the years 1993–2001 is thus likely to be even lower than the growth rate average for 1993–2000.)

Rapid economic growth is limited to but a few, and not always the same, countries. With world growth slowing, there are at any given time only a few places where wealth is being created and markets are humming, where firms can penetrate new markets and exploit new technologies. Because these boom locales change unpredictably, firms must be global to be in the right place at the right time.

Because much of the world economy is being restructured, growth is also much more rapid in some businesses than in others. Even in stagnant economies, some industries are continuing to grow through sales abroad while others are in decline because foreign firms are replacing local producers.

Law is also converging in many countries. The general rule is that of home country territoriality—that is, national law applies. But the past decade has seen a convergence internationally of laws pertaining to contracts, product liability, employee rights, and security regulations.

Procedural aspects, however, continue to differ. American law has traditionally differed from that of most of the world in that it:

- **relies on juries;**
- **permits contingency fees;**
- **does not require the loser to pay the winner's legal fees (the so-called "American rule");**
- **employs a pretrial discovery system;**

- permits class action suits; and
- awards punitive damages.

The principal remaining differences, with much of U.S. law being widely emulated abroad, are the jury system, punitive damages, and the American rule.

Firms generally favor the convergence of law because it makes it easier to operate abroad. What differences do remain, however, present opportunities to forum shop (that is, arbitrage in the law).

the backlash against globalization

The worst news for business is that there is in many countries a mounting reaction against various aspects of globalization. Its source is those who, alarmed by the speed of change wrought by globalization, are rallying to the defense of the status quo, economic or social, in their region of the globe. Many who greeted globalization with enthusiasm are retreating out of mounting concerns over what it means for their jobs and cultures.[2]

Because America is perceived in many quarters to be the most ardent proponent of globalization, the backlash against it has thus far been directed largely against Americans—their popular culture and military strength. But there is also within America significant pressure to withdraw from the global marketplace, to retreat into isolationism.[3] In other parts of the world the influence of other global powers—China and Japan, for example—is being resisted.

Business leaders tend not to recognize the significance of this backlash. Viewing the merits of the free market to be self-evident and efforts to oppose it to be not only wrong-headed, but self-defeating, they are inclined to dismiss the phenomenon. Opposition to globalization is more than sour grapes and its influence could be profound.

In many parts of the globe, globalization sits like a thin skin over a deeper culture steeped in local social and political morés. In a sense, it is like the crust on the Earth floating over the hot, shifting mantle. When an explosion in the magma of culture and civilization breaks through the crust, ordinary business is swept away.

globalization versus globalism

Appreciation for the distinction between globalization and globalism (see Figure 2-1) is crucial to an understanding of how the world is changing at the beginning of the twenty-first century. Globalization is a corporate phenomenon; globalism, a national phenomenon. A global enterprise is a "citizen of the world"; it does not rely on any one country for capital, revenues, or employees. (In contrast, a multinational company usually considers itself to have a home country from which to draw cultural context, a large portion of top management, and perhaps even most shareholders.) Globalism relates to the international spread of ideas, lifestyles, social morés, religions, fads, or

Globalism	Globalization
• A phenomenon of nations.	• A phenomenon of companies.
• The degree to which one country's ideas, fashions, or lifestyles influence people in another country.	• The degree to which a company operates in a global, as opposed to a national or multinational, framework.
• The notion of a single dominant culture emerging in most or all countries.	• The notion of a company as a "citizen of the world."

Figure 2-1 Globalism versus Globalization

political movements. When such diffusion is occurring, globalism can be said to be advancing; when it is not, globalism can be said to be retreating.[4]

Although they differ, globalism and globalization are related in that the active proponents of globalization are often perceived to act as agents of globalism. If one views globalism, as many of its opponents do, as a virus, nondomestic enterprises are one of its prime carriers. Disney's expansion theme parks in Japan and France, for example, carry with them significant elements of American culture, just as French, German, and Italian wines shipped to the United States carry with them significant elements of European culture. Because globalization contributes greatly to globalism, those opposed to globalism often oppose globalization as well.

It is sometimes difficult to distinguish cause and effect. Opposition to globalism reflects concerns for identity—cultural, social, and national; opposition to globalization, economic insecurity. Which is dominant? Is globalism the boogey man and globalization attacked as its agent? Or is the culture of commercial opponents attacked to try to gain economic advantage? For one threatened by globalization, globalism is a convenient target—not only the foreign product, but the foreign culture, is attacked as well.

As with any major change in the world, misfortunes have been attributed to globalization. Lagging local competitiveness typically begets transitory unemployment and declining wages. Worried by the poor environmental records and inadequate social safety nets of developing world nations, people in the developed world clamor for protection from globalization and from an emerging globalism rooted in third-world standards. Proponents of globalization quite rationally argue that such fears are unfounded.

sources of backlash

economic dislocation

Globalization has been attended by a change in the nature of the economies of industrialized nations variously reflected in: a shift from manufacturing to services; an explosion of new technology and the emergence of great new firms; demands for new workforce skills; jobs being lost and created in the transition. The timing of the transition is less than perfect. Unemployment rises for a while, then, if the transition is successful, falls. Globalization is the author of considerable change and dislocation.

In America the transition to the global economy is well under way, one might even say completed for the moment. Previously high American unemployment rates have fallen; inflation is tamed; real income is beginning to rise. The proportion of the workforce employed in manufacturing has declined substantially. The largest firms have seen their proportion of total employment more than halved (from 20 percent in 1960 to 9 percent in 1997) as they have struggled to improve productivity to meet foreign competition.

Initially these changes increased unemployment, but subsequent expansion of the service sector has more than offset lost manufacturing jobs. Moreover, small- and medium-sized firms have expanded employment to more than offset job losses in large firms. Although the jobs lost in manufacturing and large firms were initially better in terms of pay levels, benefits, and employment security than those that replaced them, such is no longer the case. The jobs now being created (especially in computer technology) are by and large better than those being lost. In fact, so strong is the U.S. economy that both manufacturing and large firms are now adding jobs at the growth rate of the economy as a whole.

With this difficult transition largely behind them, Americans to a large degree accept globalization as a benign phenomenon, a route to the creation of wealth on an enormous scale. In the world as a whole Americans see globalization as promoting economic growth and encouraging democracy.

On the other hand, Americans see opposition to globalization arising out of the adverse affect of increasing world trade on a nation's established interests and the failure of such nations to make the needed economic transition in their economies. This view is not far afield; in much of the rest of the world, the transition is only beginning. People see the coming pain, but not the ultimate benefit.

France seems to Americans an extreme case, a nation in which nostalgia for a brilliant past disrupts adjustment to the present. Americans have tended to view the outcome of French elections and implicit rejection of free markets as nothing less than the nation's consignment to the status of economic backwater. "I can't believe what the French are doing," many Americans say. "But if that's the way they want to go, then let them. Their economy will suffer and ultimately they'll have to join the system." This view, however comforting, is myopic. The French are not alone in having difficulty with present trends.

There is sufficient fuel in the fireplace of economic dislocation to spark conflagrations in many countries. In Japan, for example, efforts to reform the economy by introducing more competitive markets are widely seen as sacrificing the broader interests of society to American-style globalization. Will the large classes of losers created by trade in countries beset by economic dislocation effectively stall globalization?

financial crises

As a general rule new markets are unstable. Such is the case with the currency markets in less developed nations. It makes no sense to blame governments for this inherent uncertainty and volatility. Financial crises more often have their origins in currency and share markets than in bailing into or out of mismanagement of the economy. There was, for example, little the Indonesian government could have done differently to avoid the currency turmoil of the fall of 1997.

Markets are unstable in many developing countries in part because statistics about capital account, foreign investment, and so forth are poor. Although current account data are usually adequate, Indonesia, for example, a few years ago found an entire category of imports not in the data. Because this increased the current account deficit with no comparable series going backward, it seemed that the current account had suddenly worsened greatly.

When the developed nations sponsor a market system, volatility is a necessary consequence, not merely a consequence of errors of the implementing country. Those who suffer from the volatility of global markets become their opponents.

political crises

Even if economies that have suffered financial crises recover in time, as Mexico's has done and East Asia's might do, there remains the problem of political disasters for the governments in power. Mexico's ruling party of 70 years lost its grip on the legislature and mayoralty of the capital city and its control of the presidency is threatened. The government of the Czech Republic has fallen; a Thai prime minister has been put out of a job and political turmoil is increasing in other East Asian nations.

Thus is the backlash showing itself in rising political instability; in trade blocs that seem to be, but are in fact the antithesis of, progress towards globalization; and in hidden

agendas by which countries overtly support trade liberalization, but work against it behind the scenes.

american culture and social pathology

The United States itself harbors more than a whisper of resistance to globalization. Americans who continue to fear
that jobs are leaving the United States in favor of lower-wage
foreign labor pools influence the U.S. Congress's attitude towards trade and investment liberalization (such as NAFTA),
despite studies that suggest foreign competition for jobs has
little or no influence on the U.S. economy.[5] To the contrary,
the research shows much stronger competition between
workers in low-wage countries than with American workers.
It also finds job increases abroad, consistent with U.S. job
growth in the mid-1990s, to be complementary to those in
the United States. Yet economic commentators continue to
cite foreign competition for jobs as a restraining factor in
U.S. employment and wage growth. "We can expect . . . se-
vere downward pressure on wages in the industrialized
world," wrote a former undersecretary of Commerce in the
Clinton administration.[6]

The backlash outside of the United States against globalization has roots not only in concern about job loss and economic dislocation, but also in the American cultural
invasion. American popular culture is proving to be a
much-desired commodity in the countries to which it is
being exported via motion pictures, television shows, popular music, and the Internet. It is surprising, in fact, just

how popular American culture can be outside of the United States. Japan and France—the sites of Disney's international theme parks—are known to have strong pervasive national cultures, yet Mickey Mouse has conquered both. Disneyland Tokyo is the world's most popular theme park and Disneyland Paris, although greeted with disdain by French intellectuals, attracts more than 11 million visitors annually, making it by far the most popular tourist attraction in France.[7] Brands that carry American culture— Coca-Cola, McDonald's, Pepsi, IBM, and Marlboro as well as Disney—are strong worldwide.

But American culture is not always welcome. To some, its contents are offensive; to others, the social pathology thought to be its companion, is offensive. America has a reputation for crime, drugs, violence, racial and ethnic discrimination, greed on an enormous scale, and a lack of community cohesiveness. These negative elements of American life are believed to be linked to American popular culture, as suggested by the recent celebration of the heroin culture in America's fashion magazines. Technology seems to be placing all the world at the doorstep of American culture. "No spot on earth will be Microsoft-free" read the headline over a column in a leading British paper.[8]

It can hardly come as a surprise that many countries' leaders would prefer to avoid these unattractive features of American life by excluding American popular culture. The political leadership of Singapore has been particularly outspoken in this regard.

Fear of economic decline from global competition and the undermining of national culture and standards of behavior can fuel a resistance to globalism that can find striking expression.

"If market forces are allowed [unfettered reign], it will spell the end of civilization in Western Europe," proclaimed French premier Lionel Jospin to the European Socialist Congress in Malmo.[9] The connection between market economics and an apocalyptic view of society's future can be understood only in a context in which globalization is seen as the leading edge of American cultural domination. Hence, the fervor of the backlash.

Fear of job loss, economic dislocation, and resistance to American popular culture and the social pathology it is believed to engender are the foundations of the backlash against globalization.

the logic of globalization

Despite an internal logic—involving trade, capital markets, and geopolitics—globalization is being resisted, in one way or another, by every major country. Developed nations are resisting the economic logic of growing trade and economic dislocations that ensue. The welfare state was created to cushion the affect of economic change, yet the market weakens the state's ability to provide security. This has led many people to rethink the concept of government—if it is not to protect people, then what is it for? This is a clash of political desire (the welfare state) and economic competition (trade and technology).

Opposition to free markets is strongly expressed. "People expect the state to take the initiative or at least pick up the

pieces," writes Tony Judt. "Because global markets do exist
. . . and much of what happens in people's lives today has
passed from their control or the control of those who govern
them, there is a greater need than ever to hold on to the
sorts of intermediate institutions that make possible normal
civilized life."[10]

The call for state-guaranteed normalcy that rings loudly
in Europe today calls to mind an incident that occurred several years ago in the United States. One of a group of managers meeting General Electric Company's top executive,
Jack Welch, remarked: "We've been reorganizing and restructuring and downsizing. We know this is necessary to
regain our position in international competition, but when
will we return to normal?" It was a powerful question, expressing clearly the longing in many hearts for a return to a
more secure economy. But Welch answered with a question
of his own: "What makes you think that what we've been
going through isn't normal?" Turmoil and insecurity being
the new normalcy of the global economy, the collision of
great firms in the international marketplace and its logic,
there is little wonder many people long for protection.

Less-developed countries are resisting the financial logic
of the global capital markets which demand a certain degree
of predictability and government financial responsibility.
Governments that act independently of established wisdom
cannot be tolerated. When financial market psychology turns
negative, there is a call to cut back economic activity to facilitate financial stability. Developing countries, perceiving this
to be a substantial price to pay, resist it.

The world superpower, the United States, seems in some
ways to resist the political logic of its own position, both

sponsoring free markets and globalization and pursuing domestic interests as if it were merely a participant. Consequently, it is seen to profit from a global economic system that discomfits many. It seems to rig the global game and succeed whatever occurs. Political logic dictates that to sustain support for globalization, the United States must use its political clout to mitigate its rigors for others. That it does so only to a small degree is a source of rising resistance to the system it sponsors.

how other countries should respond

That a backlash against globalization exists in nearly every country is understandable, but resistance is not the most constructive response. Developed countries would benefit from freer and more flexible economies that would speed, smooth, and minimize the cost of the transitions required by globalization. Developing countries would benefit from greater regulation of financial institutions and more transparency in business and financial activities. The United States, in particular, would benefit from less aggressive promotion of its social and economic system and greater sensitivity to the concerns of others in its pursuit of domestic and global objectives.

It would be well if such positive responses to the challenges of globalization prevailed, but it is likely that they will not, in which case executives will have to contend, as best they can, with a world coming apart at the geopolitical level even as it is bound ever more tightly at the technological level. The potential in the resulting tension is being more effectively exploited by firms than by nations, which is why economic growth is so anemic in many parts of the globe. The issue for firms has become: How to take advantage of global opportunities when nations are not?

points to remember

- The e-Leader prepares for the good news and bad news about the world economy which is ahead.

- Globalization and electronic commerce are coupling to create the business world of the future.

- Firms must change how they do business in a networked world.

  The virtual world will change how firms are structured and how people interact.

  Electronic commerce will change the businesses firms are in.

- The trend towards globalization has benefited the United States, but a backlash against globalization is gaining strength.

- In anticipation of a more uncertain political climate in the world, e-Leaders must focus on achieving greater speed in adjustments.

CHAPTER 3

identifying
business arrays

THE E-LEADER RECOGNIZES THAT VALUE CREATION BEGINS
with perceiving and pursuing opportunities. In large companies this effort is the role of the corporate strategy group.
But corporate strategy remains an overly centralized, time-
consuming process and lacks a conceptual framework appropriate to contemporary business settings. This chapter
addresses the latter shortcoming; the former is considered
in Chapter 9.

Industry being too large, the firm too small, a concept on
which to base strategy—the struggle is on to discover a
conceptual framework that lies between the two.

Two concepts are being advanced to fill the gap: the
value-chain and the cluster of firms. Both are useful: Both
derived from the production side of business. The value-
chain, which defines the sequence of activities by which a
product or service is brought to the market, is of more
recent origin. The cluster, which describes a group of customers and suppliers in geographic proximity to one another, has been applied for years in a variety of constructive

ways. Central to both concepts is how a firm seeks to maximize productivity and minimize costs in meeting an established market demand.

Business is currently evolving in such a way that the greatest value-creation lies in establishing new products and services by calling into existence new value-chains and clusters. What remains unclear is how to conceptualize the early stages of new sectors of the economy before the emergence of value-chains and clusters.

A useful analogy is the physics of the first few moments of the universe, of the so-called Big Bang. The physics of the period of creation is very different from that of the established universe. We live in the established universe and are familiar with its rules; when we try to comprehend the period of creation, we find it bizarre.

Managers seeking a conceptual framework to guide them through the early stages of the twenty-first century must stretch their minds, think outside of established mental boxes, and accept ideas that initially might seem peculiar. These ideas must not be rejected because they don't comport with our current notions. A source for a new framework may well be as near as the world of high technology and the Internet, but only if we view it without strong preconceptions.

enter the business array

Although it has come to the fore in our thinking because of its centrality in Internet space, the business array is a difficult notion for traditional executives whose templates for it are few—it's neither an industry nor a value-chain, nor a legal form—like a joint venture or partnership. Instead, it's a framework for strategic design in the early stages of development of a new economic sector.

Emerging concepts are often best explained by means of examples, including the Internet firms discussed briefly in Chapter 1. Collegetown.usa was founded to assist college-bound students with the process of selecting and gaining acceptance at a school. The company has developed a network of some 135 schools' "infosites" that makes available student guides and links to area businesses, services, and facilities.

Awareness that many other firms were engaged in developing the Internet as a place to do business is what led Collegetown.usa's founders to prospect this space. Generation of sufficient traffic to ensure financial viability was assured by the plethora of other firms providing Internet-based services to college students and their parents. Collegetown.usa's expansion of services has been largely through partnerships and alliances, such as with Monsterboard (which provides content for its career center) and New Promise, Inc. (which provides a database of college courses that can be taken by students over the Internet). Relationships with some of its partners are formal, involving contracts; with others, informal, based on agreements. Even more casual relationships include links to sites offering complementary services and the very activities of the firms establishing and trying to cultivate customers for such sites.

Collegetown has become embedded in an array of firms and individuals collectively trying to extract value from a set of complementary services delivered via the Internet. (It has competitors, which are in different arrays but often overlap, having some members in common.) Collegetown's array is not its industry, which is much larger; nor does it in any way dominate its array. Collegetown is very much aware of the other players in its array, which it views as collaborators in the creation and rivals in the capture of value therefrom.

the array as concept for strategy

In today's world, strategy is about how to position one's firm in an array in such a way as to develop brand recognition and then move on to capture a disproportionate amount of the value created by the array as a whole. Organization design is about how to create a firm that can do this. Building a culture is about energizing the firm to capture value. Operations are about speeding decision-making and execution to seize value.

An array is a concept in strategy based in customer space. It is not so much firms working together to produce a product or service as firms working in parallel to create value by meeting customer needs through a variety of related (both loosely and integrally) products and services. The term's dictionary definition is instructive.[1] It is a transitive verb meaning "to set out for use; to place in an orderly arrangement."

As a noun, it is defined as "1. An orderly, often imposing arrangement. 2. An impressively large number, as of persons or objects. 3. Splendid attire. 4. Mathematics: an arrangement of quantities in rows or columns as in a matrix. 5. Computer science: an arrangement of memory elements in one or several planes."

An array is not an organization. The dictionary defines an organization as "a structure through which individuals cooperate systematically to conduct business; the administrative personnel of such a structure," and therein lies the distinction. At the core of an organization is an administrative structure, a bureaucracy. At the core of an array is a purpose, a focus around which individuals and units align themselves and towards which they work. To object as one might, that a bureaucracy has a purpose as well, is to ignore the issue. An organization is, above all, an administrative structure, which—if the experience of this century is any guide—has an inherent propensity to substitute self perpetuation for whatever its original purpose might have been.

Administrative structure claims executives' time and attention. Its need for continual review and modification keeps them directed inward towards their firms' bureaucracies. Executives whose firms participate in an array continually refine their focus in its context: an outward-directed activity focused on opportunities.

mapping the array

As said previously, an array is the marketplace neighborhood of a firm—the locale in which it gets its brand established and determines its relationships with customers. Consultants must analyze three aspects of this neighborhood to put the array into operation:

- **the customers to be served**
- **the "other" companies that co-exist in the customer neighborhood**
- **the processes and activities performed in serving these customers**

Skilled consultants can tap industry and company data to study the appropriate customer bases, assess the competitive or cooperative posture of the other companies in the relative neighborhood, and then specify the processes and activities that must be performed to deliver value to the chosen customers. These data, captured in answer to the following eight questions asked of client executives, industry analysts, and end customers, are used to specify an array map:

1. **Who are the real customers to be served?**
2. **What value do these customers receive?**
3. **Which are the major firms attempting to serve these customers?**
4. **What is each firm offering?**
5. **What processes are performed to deliver this value?**
6. **Which of these processes are "core" or "enabling"?**
7. **Where are the activities within each core process that really add value?**
8. **How much value is gained or lost by "owning" each of these levers?**

Why questions one and two? In an environment where industry, geography, or product have lost solidity, customers remain a beacon. Why questions three and four? Array analysts must know which other companies are available to serve as prospective partners in the client's array or which must be countered lest they come together to form a competing array in opposition to the client. Why questions five through eight? Tactical decisions about which activities a company should provide to its array must be informed by an understanding of which activities generate the greatest value for their provider.

Why is it so important to return to the "first principles" implied in these basic strategic questions? The wired world imposes a new degree of connectivity on business. Yesterday's technology automated processes and tightened linkages without affecting boundaries. Today's technology, by enhancing communication inside and across companies, is blurring company boundaries. In a wired world it is not clear where one company begins and another ends.

As company boundaries blur, market and industry boundaries follow. Relationships between companies and customers are transformed. Companies that once satisfied customers on their own must seek partners to deliver solutions more efficiently. Companies that never crossed paths find themselves working the same customer base, and companies pushed out of one value-chain must join others to prosper. (A coffee vendor like Starbucks can open kiosks in Barnes & Noble stores; even as Barnes & Noble partners with publisher Bertlesmann to go online—hoping to eliminate its physical outlets!)

customers

One cliché about the wired world is that customers can access much information. However, too much information may be as bad for choice as too little once was. This is why portal sites—shortcuts for customers to vendors[2]—have appeared. But behind these info-mediaries is an even more interesting marketing phenomenon. Where firms were once product directed, pushing wares at customers, they are now becoming "intentions" directed, getting customers to pull their wares into the marketplace.

companies

Understanding which companies must be accounted for as prospective competitors or are available to serve as collaborators when mapping an array is a subtle art. The old dynamics of value-chains have limited applicability in the wired world. Your best collaborator can become your worst enemy and former enemies can become friends.

It is still possible to use the existing tools for analyzing strategic advantage such as analysis of core competence, market-share figures, or the growth-experience curve. Whichever combination of specific tools is used to identify the companies of the neighborhood, the resulting template should look somewhat like Figure 3-1.

The data in Figure 3-1 comes from the computer industry. The vertical stovepipe companies of the mainframe have become the loosely integrated layers of the PC. Where a few large vendors pushed integrated solutions into the market,

Activities

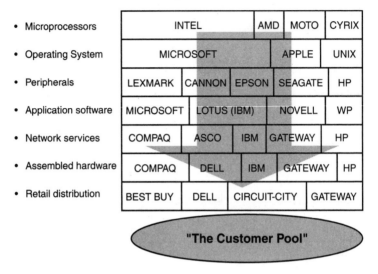

- Microprocessors
- Operating System
- Peripherals
- Application software
- Network services
- Assembled hardware
- Retail distribution

INTEL		AMD	MOTO	CYRIX
MICROSOFT		APPLE		UNIX
LEXMARK	CANNON	EPSON	SEAGATE	HP
MICROSOFT	LOTUS (IBM)		NOVELL	WP
COMPAQ	ASCO	IBM	GATEWAY	HP
COMPAQ	DELL	IBM	GATEWAY	HP
BEST BUY	DELL	CIRCUIT-CITY		GATEWAY

"The Customer Pool"

Figure 3-1 The PC Industry

many small companies now compete and collaborate to achieve similar ends. No one company can deliver a complete PC; the industry space is occupied by a jungle of partnerships, technology agreements, and groupings around industry standards.

There are multiple arrays active among the companies in Figure 3-1. Intel and Microsoft—plus selected assemblers and retailers—offer IBM-compatible PCs. Motorola and Apple, plus certain retailers, offer the Macintosh. Dell, plus component makers (now including IBM), offer made-to-order PCs through the Internet—bypassing retailers. A grouping of Motorola, Apple, and IBM offered the Power-PC chip in competition with Intel's family of x86 processors, and many companies are now exploring LINUX as an alternative to MS-Windows.

processes and activities

Process/activities analysis provides granularity to the emerging array map. This helps client executives observe and target particularly desirable addresses in the neighborhood. For example, Coca-Cola Inc. has created an array in which it provides the formula (Coke syrup) and brand management, thereby greatly leveraging the millions of tons of sugar and water, and many millions of dollars' worth of bottling plant, provided by its 42 partly owned bottling affiliates.

Process/activities analysis proceeds in three steps. First, the enabling processes are isolated from the core processes. While enabling processes must still be performed, they are not strategic and can be assigned to outsourcing vendors without the consideration given to core process providers.[3]

Second, the core processes are disaggregated into value-adding steps and related "make or buy" decisions. This is done to create a preliminary partner shopping list; to help ascertain what prospective partners might be doing out in the marketplace; and how they could help deliver value to the emerging array. (As a rule of thumb: If a company can buy output from one step and sell input to the next step, a market can be inserted between the steps.)

Third, each step is deconstructed into critical activities—the nitty-gritty of operations. This yields activities that yield greater value to those who perform them because they perform them more efficiently. Sizing these activities requires estimation. At best, activity-based costing (ABC) techniques applied to industry accounting data can be used to get solid numbers; at worst, analysts will have to resort to "rule of thumb" high, medium, or low projections.[4]

tactics: choosing which activities to perform

Consultants or executives use the array-map to answer tactical questions about participation.

1. Which activities do I want my company to perform?

2. Which ones do I want another company to perform?

Thinking through these issues is a two-step effort. First, the investment required for each activity must be assessed in light of present company core competencies. Second, these requirements must be compared to indications of value on the array map. It is important to note that not every company will see small activities as no-go zones, because they are particularly well suited to perform the activity sited at these points and will accept small scale. Some, too, will perceive larger activities being closed to them because they do not have suitable competencies to deliver them in an economic fashion. The following rules can help classify the opportunities:

- If I don't have the critical competencies to perform any activity on the array map without investing heavily, I should stop. This customer opportunity is not suitable for me.

- If I have the critical competencies to perform at least one activity without investing heavily, I should use that activity as my entry point to the array. While an activity yielding limited value is less interesting than one yielding great value, I could build a limited position into a larger one over time. (As Microsoft and Intel did with IBM—remember both were "invited" to help IBM with its PC!)

- If I can build critical competencies for an activity with moderate investment and attention, then I must ask: (1) If the activity is a large one, do I sacrifice short-run returns to enter this array? and (2) If the activity is a small one, can I afford to wait out limited returns and grow with the activity? (Both choices require analysis of the other opportunities available to the company.)

There are some further principles of participation that should be noted in passing:

- While some activities are clearly not so lucrative as others, all activities must be performed to deliver value. This opens up possible combinations. Also some companies may have to absorb a lesser activity to secure a greater one because no one else will.

- It is possible for more than one company to perform a specific activity, particularly in a geographic context where companies provide input across unique territories. Thus, a company should not panic if it sees an erstwhile competitor chasing one of "its" activities; opportunities can be divided.

- Different levels of participation yield different degrees of influence. While a disproportionate share of value typically accrues to companies with greater roles, the bigger players also perform the costly administrative tasks of building culture, harmonizing systems, and creating the governance infrastructure required for coherent operation.

points to remember

- A business array is a value-creating concept in strategy that includes firms building related products and services for consumers.

- Arrays, most common in the development of new products and services, often indicate the emergence of a new industry.

- Arrays include not only firms that have contractual business relationships, but also firms that are simply working in the same general direction. The firms in an array sometimes compete, but more often work together or in parallel.

building a
global lattice

The e-Leader must develop a way of assembling resources and organizing them in the value space that carries forward today's network organization. The most promising approach is the lattice—the next generation of the global network.

CHAPTER 4

defining a
global lattice

KNOWLEDGE WORKERS NOW PROVIDE THE BULK OF VALUE creation to businesses of the new economy, and most of them think of themselves as professionals, whether or not they have advanced degrees and whether or not they are members of one of the traditional professions such as law, medicine, engineering, or architecture. But the little discussed secret of knowledge workers is that generally they don't work very well together in close physical proximity: There are too many big egos that rub abrasively against one another. The close teamwork among computer engineers in a skunk works when building a new machine is unusual; the close cooperation among consultants in a single room when fashioning a proposal to a client for a new engagement is unusual.

In fact, professionals work better together when they are at a physical distance (this is the great paradox—the distance paradox—of professional teamwork) and modern communications make it possible for the paradox to be employed often and on a large scale. Teams of professionals at distant locations using the Internet or corporate intranets to communicate, share working documents, or work simultaneously on documents are the most productive of teams today. It's not despite the distance among their members—it's because of it.

What has been needed is an organizational approach that recognizes the paradox of professional cooperation—it is often better to have greater physical distance among the people—and that facilitates long-distance cooperation. This is the objective, the mission, of the lattice.

E-Leaders recognize that the distance paradox is the reason why even large and powerful companies operating in the traditional manner are likely to be outperformed by groups of smaller firms operating as global lattices. In success, if not in numbers, the lattice is likely to become the dominant form of organization because it best harnesses the power of professional teamwork.

designing a global lattice

How should firms be configured to seize opportunities created by the new economics? The most common answer today is the network organization. To consulting gurus and executives alike, the network presents a beguiling symmetry; in defining both a technological construct and a form of human interaction, the term implies that the technical and human organization are somehow synchronized, a false implication.

The technological infrastructure that supports both firms and the global marketplace is rapidly outpacing the capability of the human organization. Those bedazzled and befuddled by the pace of change are inclined to impose subtle restraints on it. This is why knowledge sharing is not working well in large firms and why, consequently, even the best companies are failing to effectively extend their global reach. Many firms have established knowledge exchanges, but their knowledge workers aren't sharing. What is crucial is to bring knowledge to the action point, be it Kuala Lumpur or Paris. Today, no location is farther than an e-mail message from any other.

The failing of the network organization is that it does not match the human and technological organization of firms and the marketplace. The lattice is an alternative to the organization, neither hierarchy nor network, but a formal structure comprising connected elements that can be extensively customized to meet specific applications. The business array, a strategic concept, has organizational implications; it leads to the lattice, a concept in organizational design. A step beyond the network organization, the lattice imposes order on the former's loose protocols.

Executives and consultants have for many decades pursued global organization by stitching together products, functions, and countries guided by studies of the relative economics of locating a plant in one country over another. The global lattice, an entity that comprises firms no one of which owns it or controls its entirety, provides an alternative structure for pursuing globalization. No longer does being global mean having to put some part of a firm in a number of different countries. The global lattice has a presence in every location occupied by its constituent firms; it achieves global reach not through ownership of, but rather through a commonality across, multiple locations.

A lattice is perhaps most easily understood in contrast to a task force, a collection of organizational elements assembled to pursue a short-term, limited objective. A lattice is a scaled-up task force. To shift to a military analogy, it is equivalent to the disposition of units deployed for a campaign. A headquarters is established and units are assigned to it. The units might be drawn from different services or from different organizational elements of the same service (for example, army, naval, and air force units, or divisions, regimental teams and special purpose unit elements within the army). Each element has its own home in the continuing, permanent organization of the army, navy or air force, but each is now assigned a role in the headquarters theatre command. This is analogous to a business array. Note that the latter is far more substantial than a task force—its mission is broad; its time frame, lengthy; its resources, significant.

Whether used for arranging the design of tiles, wall paper, or a stand to support climbing plants (a sort of trellis), a lattice formally has two-dimensional symmetry—length and width.[1] A lattice organization has two dimensions of symmetry as well: geographic and time, so that the lattice is not merely a patchwork of always varying relationships and structures (an organizational chaos, so to speak), but instead has repetitive elements; it's an organization design. Repeated elements involve geographic combinations and combinations that occur, disappear, and reoccur over time. In other words, a firm is likely to repeat certain combinations of resources in a valuable pattern geographically, and also to repeat them over time to deal with emerging opportunities and problems.

A global lattice might be likened to a telescopic array: the clustered antennae of a radio telescope. The very large array (VLA) makes use of a key principle in the physics of radio waves: It is not necessary to build ever-larger antennae to improve granularity of observation through a radio telescope. By focusing many small dishes—each with a unique perspective—on the same object, and using advanced signal processing to adjust for the differing perspectives of each dish, astronomers can generate detailed radiograms without building giant antennae.

As a dish collects signals from space, so the elements of a lattice gather market information. This information is then deployed in decision-making through the business equivalent of advanced signal processing. The capacity of each element of the lattice, like that of each telescope dish, is limited. Only when the elements of the lattice are focused on the same opportunity in the global economy— as telescopic dishes are focused on the same object in space—is the full value-creation potential of the combination realized.

The very large telescopic array and organizational lattice share a number of key characteristics, among them:

- multiple independent components;
- operation along several dimensions;
- communication with a central hub; and
- universal focus on the same objective.

This is a very different model from that promoted in recent years under the label of network organization. The lattice resembles a central hub system. The network organization places less emphasis on a center and more on lateral connections, some proponents going so far as to sponsor a centerless corporation. The latter, although an option for business organization in the new century, is a less attractive one than an organization with a strong, but neither controlling nor autocratic, center.

That more advanced global enterprises are configuring themselves around business processes rather than reporting relationships, divisions, or departments—the traditional elements of organization—facilitates the use of the lattice as an organizational device. The lattice has only minimal formal structure, is not chaotic, and achieves regularity and predictability through:

- a common infrastructure for information management and knowledge exchange;

- a common culture or "global mindset";

- strict use of the logic of market forces (each unit performs well-defined tasks and has distinct but not captive buyers); and

- consistent use of economic value measurement criteria (management knows how much value is being created by each activity within each business process).

Traditionally, companies that went abroad relied on hierarchical principles to maintain headquarters' control over activities, an approach that created layer upon layer of country managers, regional managers, and support staffs at each level. Recognizing that local responsiveness was blunted by centralization, executives pruned away middle management and ended up with myriad local divisions, an approach that enhanced local responsiveness at the expense of efficient resource deployment and information flows eroding profitability through duplication of effort. A global network resolves the choice between responsiveness and efficiency by enabling managers to effectively deploy information technologies to reduce the complexity inherent in global operations.

A would-be global enterprise need no longer duplicate countless functions and resources around the world because now it can install multipoint information systems that store data only once and transmit and transform as necessary for global use. This is a vital development because it is not organization structure, but the flow and transformation of information into knowledge and the actions that knowledge triggers that are important. Organization structure is merely a vehicle for transferring information from its point of creation or interception to where it is to be used. The more efficiently and effectively a firm can do this, the more competitive it will be.

A lattice accommodates knowledge flow without extensive managerial intermediation. The notion of delegation among organization layers is antiquated. Arrays, being essentially flat, avoid delegation. A representative of a Prague-based company that is part of a global network exercises the decision and action authority of the array itself; he or she is the array in Prague. Such an individual must consequently be competent, well-motivated, and able to draw effectively on array resources including global information stockpiles, worldwide.

The lattice thus unleashes human potential. But as important as getting to people information that enables them to act quickly is to guard against information overload. A mechanism must exist to prioritize information, to determine which should be acted upon and which deferred. This is the function of hierarchy. A lattice substitutes for the hierarchy of authority a hierarchy of information. Elements of a lattice take direction from their information and communication systems, not from organizational superiors. The same system that cranks out an operating report for a process manager located in a geographically distant country and in the heart of the lattice can deliver a report incorporating the same information to the CEO at headquarters. Effective leadership in a lattice follows information, knowledge, skills, and relationships rather than position, title, or rank.

The next logical step from hierarchy and conventional network, the lattice overcomes the limitations of and gains power from both:

- **the power of definition and structural strength from hierarchies of information and leadership; and**
- **the power of flexibility from networks.**

A global network possesses a unique combination of qualities that enables its participants to seize global opportunities. Specifically, it is both:

- **dynamic (the lattice's relatively fluid composition and reliance on market forces facilitates the formation and reformation of required relationships) and**
- **value-focused (the lattice's focus on processes drives value creation).**

Dynamism is dictated by today's fast-moving business environment, in which managers must constantly seek better, faster, more efficient ways to perform essential tasks, as by changing vendors, alliance partners, or suppliers as economic value moves around the globe or the value-map of the array. A value-focus is needed to facilitate the application of economic value discipline and generate responsiveness to changing conditions.

Participation in a global lattice at once enables a firm to take advantage of business opportunities outside its core competencies and prevents the firm overreaching in a global environment fraught with difficulties for conventionally organized entitles that tend to be too big, too slow moving, and too risk adverse.

Perhaps the most important competence of a global lattice is the knowledge-exchange capability that supports geographic dispersion and enables perpetual integration in the array. It is this capability that enables a lattice to cohere whether its activity teams are co-located or dispersed around the world. A global network speeds information flow and decision-making by assigning significant authority to activity teams and routing vital data directly to them. Middle managers are no longer the sole official medium for information flow; the lattice flattens the classic management pyramid into a disk with rings. But redistribution for authority is not absence of authority. A core team of executives drawn from producer and ally companies remains responsible for strategic intent, key investments, team missions, performance measurement, and alliance relationships. A lattice's core team has the potential to exercise greater authority than its traditional company counterpart because it has access to all elements of an array. But because activity teams are empowered to access these same elements on their own initiative, exercise of this authority is generally not extensive.

A lattice's global network supports three distinct knowledge-exchange capabilities:

- **among core team managers who exchange mission and measurement data;**

- **among activity teams that exchange process information via a common "infostructure"; and**

- **among activity teams' members networked to support virtual operation.**

An energized network—a high-performing human organization in which people are connected both electronically and physically in a complex quasi-formal structure and motivated by considerable freedom of association and action— is needed to seize the potential created by the new business economics. Extraneous resources and unnecessary capabilities detract from value-creation. A lattice focuses human energy and brings required capabilities (skills) to bear of selected resources (people) on a business opportunity. A lattice's flexibility; its capability to reconfigure assets, people, and activities as needed, and leverage the specialized intellectual capabilities of different firms are essential to survival and growth in today's unstable competitive environment. These resources and capabilities are given a means of coherent action by defining business processes—sequences of activities that, when performed, generate value.

Finally, a lattice spreads risk across multiple organizations, an important consideration in the development of new products and services, to which is imputed both more risk and greater value-creation than attends a simple extension of an existing set of market offerings.

the technological expression of a lattice

The aggregate of firms, business units, teams, and individuals that comprise a lattice has a technological counterpart in the extranet whereby individual firms link to their suppliers, partners, and, in some instances, customers. Lattices and extranets facilitate business by linking elements irrespective of their boundaries for specific purposes.

How does an extranet differ from the intranets and the Internet? The Internet is the collective hardware (servers, switches, telephone lines, and so forth) and software (application systems, firewalls, encryption modules, and so forth) that support communication among millions of computers worldwide. An intranet is a local collection of hardware and software that supports intrafirm communication. Making an intranet compatible with and accessible from the Internet greatly enhances a firm's flexibility. An extranet is effectively an external extension of an intranet that, for purposes of security, is generally isolated from the Internet. It accommodates electronic exchanges with specific, designated external entities (for example, suppliers, partners, customers). The massive potential for information flow that empowers employees (and powers the lattice) might be likened to a fire hose that, to be effective, must be regulated and directed by a professional firefighter. Without managers to regulate and direct it, lattice-generated information flows will flood organizations and drown efficient operations. Most firms retain substantial management but there are alternatives within the lattice. When management levels are eliminated in the interest of empowerment, managers are replaced by logic of work teams (peer discipline substitutes for supervisory oversight), market forces (buyers and suppliers substitute for management direction), and process flow (team formation is precipitated by the existence of at least one, largely self-contained, measurably, value-adding activity). The logic of these forces channels human energy into a coherent flow that energizes the lattice.

the lattice versus the traditional organization

A lattice comprises competence-based affiliates specialized to operate in their local contexts and a top layer of generalists (one can't get into the top layer without having service assignments in several parts of the world) who travel a lot.

To say that a lattice has an important element of flexibility is not to say that it is necessarily informal; in fact, it may be highly structured. Lattices generate flexibility from the general nature of their elements, which individually retain systematic procedures and protocols that they continue to follow.

Understanding this last point helps to avoid confusing structure with management style. Authoritarianism (a management style) is often associated with traditional organization (a structure); participation (a management style) with networks (a structure). It is entirely possible to have participation in a traditional organization.

The objectives of a business lattice are to cost-efficiently combine flexibility and efficiency, and be reconfigurable, specific to a purpose, and self-controlling. These are achieved by designating specific purpose units that sacrifice some flexibility in order to become highly efficient. There must also be a high degree of flexibility somewhere in the organization to accommodate adaptation of the specialized functions to different uses—that is, to support customization. In a global oil company lattice, for example, the top management layer is flexible, and the product, country, and lower levels highly specialized. (See Figure 4-1.) The cost of providing for great flexibility at all layers is—as some have suggested—too great to be an acceptable solution for most businesses.

If alliance partner teams within the process structure are considered to be external to the basic entity, then extranet links entities that contribute to the owner firm and its processes. If what the firm owns is isolated from what its alliance partners own, then we are multiple intranets (since each of the firm's alliance partners probably does the same thing it does). Opening its "firewalls" (software barriers that prevent "outsiders" from accessing its servers) renders

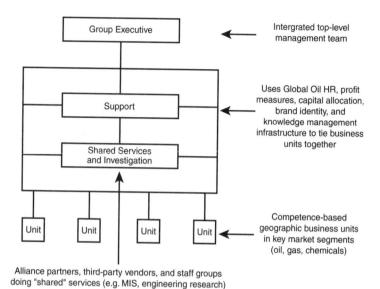

Figure 4-1 Global Oil Company Lattice

the firm part of the Internet, able to communicate with any entity that possesses an e-mail address.

The global business environment has been sufficiently stable for the past decade to permit traditional pyramid organizations to continue to flourish. Although that is now changing, it is important to recognize that the lattice is not ideally suited for application in all operating environments. The global economic environment—though generally not now chaotic, save in some regions and sectors—is nevertheless less stable than before, creating a venue of applicability for the flexible lattice structure. Figure 4-2 summarizes alternative structures for operating environments relative to degree of managerial control and market dictates.

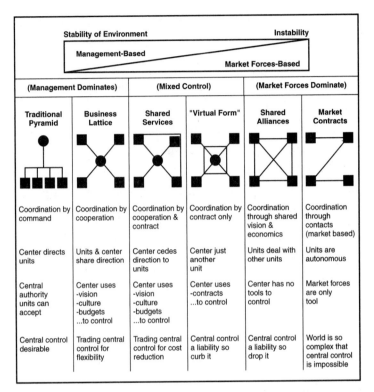

Figure 4-2 The Lattice in the Range of Organizational Relationships

Although technology has afforded the opportunity to migrate towards alternatives to managerial control (represented to the right in Figure 4-2), firms have largely chosen to retain as much managerial control as possible. The lattice is a preliminary movement towards more marketlike business arrangements. It is an important movement because it has major consequences—permitting managers to meet new business opportunities with greater flexibility and considerably more managerial control than is possible with shared services, virtual firms, or alliances.

To operate both globally and locally, firms must determine the appropriate degree of centralization and decentralization (see Figure 4-3).

The transition from the traditional centralized organization structure to one that is both decentralized and involves considerable delegation has been difficult because centralized control has so often mitigated against focus in the new environment. What has been needed is a new approach that imposes order on what has been a loose set of protocols for managing human networks in order to focus attention, improve operational efficiency, and accommodate flexible adaptation to local conditions. Figure 4-4 depicts the range of choices: from headquarters' control of most matters to very few.

Networks without sufficient structure fail because members' roles are ambiguous or ill-defined. Hierarchy doesn't help because it channels information upward away from

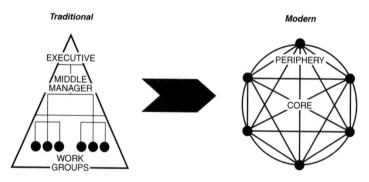

Figure 4-3 Decentralization and Delegation

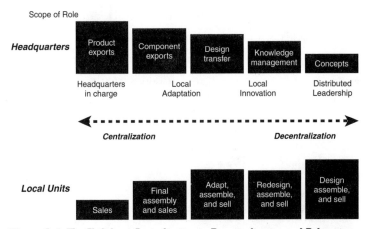

Figure 4-4 The Shift from Centralization to Decentralization and Delegation

those at the local level who need access to it in order to be able to act in a timely fashion. What is needed is to disentangle the elements of traditional hierarchy in such a way that information can be shared, and supervision and assigned responsibility retained; in other words, to decentralize without flying to pieces.

Global enterprises are just beginning to exploit information technology to support the creation of highly decentralized, minimally layered network structures capable of operating autonomously in specific markets (locally) or in concert across multiple markets (globally) as required to maximize value creation. The management of such firms is embracing the operating discipline that is driven by market forces, process alignment, shared values, knowledge databases that reside on common technology platforms, and integrative, collaborative leadership. The resulting organization is flexible, manages comprehensively, and accommodates customization. It is nonhierarchical because individual responsibility is assigned. It is not a network in the loose sense of the term because the new organization is not unstructured; its elements have clearly defined roles.

creating a lattice

Four key actions are involved in the creation of a lattice.

invigorate informal connections

Managers are supplementing formal vertical lines of communication with direct connections established and broken as needed. Layers are skipped; functions, bypassed; firm boundaries, ignored. Electronic media is substituted for voices and print communication; formal lines of communication, such as characterized pre-modem organizations, exist only on paper, it being accepted that anyone—regardless of level, specialty, or training—may communicate with anyone else in pursuit of common business objectives.

selectively despecialize employees

Managers no longer split horizontal work tasks from vertical management tasks. Employees in a lattice must increasingly become generalists, their technical training augmented with scheduling, work analysis, and even advanced problem-solving skills. This task blurring is necessary if employees working in a team environment are to be able to interpret information that flows to them and act upon it without delay incurred by having to seek advice or approval from supervisors.

invert the decision rule

Managers no longer presume that the appropriate perspective for interpreting and acting upon information is necessarily upward. The new priority is to ensure that information is used before it loses value, the new rule, that all decisions be made as close to the point of contact and action as possible, subject only to the requirement that employees seek advice when information falls outside their experience. These rules shift the locus of decision-making away from the center (top) to the periphery (bottom) of organizations.

develop asynchronous, but interdependent, activities

A typical global enterprise with active operations in North and South America, Europe, and Asia might have facilities located in all 24 time zones. The implications of this for a traditional functional organization are profound: Unless its work day becomes continuous, company executives will not have immediate (synchronous) access to all parts of the global network—not be able to use the telephone to maintain contact with every local manager. The loss of instantaneous contact between central executives and some local managers might seem insignificant, but it is not. What happens to seamless operation in a global value-chain when certain local managers are unavailable for consultation on urgent matters of operation as opposed to leisurely reviews of strategy? Sustaining interdependence in a globally dispersed or decentralized organization will come to be an enormous challenge in the years ahead unless companies design accordingly.

The solutions are twofold. Adopt a 24-hour work day to ensure that local managers are always available to headquarters, effectively turning them into shift workers. Or redesign the organization to shift sufficient power away from the center so that asynchronous communication no longer poses a problem for company operations.

Few civilian organizations appear to be gravitating towards the "shift" approach, although the military establishment has employed it effectively for decades. Some companies, primarily in financial services, are exploring the 24-hour day, moving their active business from partners in New York to Tokyo to London as these markets open and close. More companies are delegating power to local nodes in an effort to accommodate asynchronous communication.

A lattice is an effective mechanism for solving complex problems. But problem complexity does not dictate complexity in lattice; to the contrary, lattices, to be managed effectively, must be as simple as possible.

A lattice also implies a clean slate, establishing that one effectively wipes away, for the moment, the encrustation of connotations that impedes and misdirects organizational action. Management thinking must be freed of much of organizational theory, organization behavior, and organizational psychology. Valuable in its day, this accumulated wisdom has become as blinders on a horse, obscuring from view the potentialities and problems of today's rapidly changing business environment.

a process orientation

As illustrated in Figure 4-5, a lattice is constructed on a value map that details the business processes and related activities required to deliver a lattice's strategic intent. Each activity contributes more or less value depending on the size of, and strategic nature and absolute return on, the required investment.

The workflow-process approach requires that each unit generate specific outputs for an identifiable customer. Each

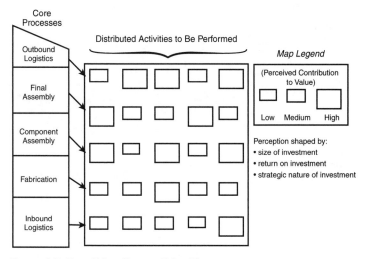

Figure 4-5 From Value-Chain to Value-Map

process is typically divisible into relative self-contained activities that can be benchmarked against equivalents elsewhere and executed by self-governing teams with limited managerial intervention.

Process division of labor is a powerful alternative to functional division of labor because it mobilizes market forces to motivate and direct people. How does it work? First, a process orientation assigns to each activity team a supplier and a customer. Each team has providers of input and buyers of output (see Figure 4-6). Beginning on the left side the three teams in closest proximity to them represent the lattice to suppliers and treat adjacent internal teams as customers. The internal teams' peers to the left are treated as suppliers; those to the right, as customers. Finally, the

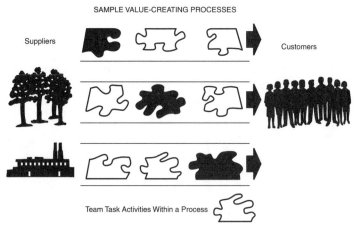

SAMPLE VALUE-CREATING PROCESSES

Suppliers

Customers

Team Task Activities Within a Process

Figure 4-6 From Value-Map to Lattice

teams closest to external customers represent the lattice to them and treat as suppliers their peers to the left.

A process orientation, moreover, makes activity output easier to measure. Consider a function (marketing) and a related process (brand management). Marketing occurs across many products; brand management is specific to brand. A manager cannot separate the value added by design or advertising decisions made simultaneously for Brand X and Brand Y. But by assigning all activities associated with Brand X to one team, costs for Brand X can be readily collected and compared with the revenues it generates.

Finally, a process orientation enables teams to share performance data. Employees deployed by function—because they seldom interact with customers or suppliers or even peers from other functions—must rely for data on managers whose perspective on the work flow is one or more levels removed. Employees deployed by process have a broader view of activity. Sustained contact with customers and suppliers yields natural performance measurements, usually as satisfaction ratings or profit criteria. Connections between buyers and sellers is immediate; unhappy buyers look to lattice management to find them new suppliers if the performance of existing suppliers cannot be brought into line with expectations.

A process orientation thus establishes a fundamental basis for effective empowerment. Each activity team has clearly defined tasks, unfiltered access to key information, and clear measures of success and failure. It is empowerment, within a context of market discipline, that generates the responsiveness companies need to compete in a fast-paced global business environment.

participating in a global lattice

A firm plays one of three key roles in a business lattice—and which one it plays is largely dependent on firm strength and management savvy. Ideally, a firm will command the role that will enable it to extract the greatest value from its participation. Often, however, a firm defaults into a less-than-ideal role because it is neither strong enough nor clever enough to secure a better one.

A firm can be one of the following:

- An *initiator* contributes key knowledge and insights or the bulk of processes or both and usually originates any changes in the direction of a lattice.

- A *player* contributes a vital process or series of linked activities.

- A *member* performs a specific activity.

The *initiator* typically provides strategic insight; provides the bulk of resources for core activities; supplies the visionaries who perceive the business opportunity (or strategic intent) that pulls lattice participants together; draws the value-map that defines the lattice's evolution; and initiates relationship negotiations and earns the lion's share of the resulting value. Because it is often entirely dependent on the business lattice for value creation, an initiator is inclined to commit substantial resources to maintain the interest of other participants in continuing to devote attention to the lattice. In a sense, the antitrust suit against Microsoft is about how Microsoft chose to compel attention from its allies and other actors in the personal computer lattice to the products from which it profited most.

> *Initiator:* supplies strategic intent, vision, and resources for major activities, and usually has a core leadership team.

A *player* typically contributes significant resources, but does not actively participate in the formulation of strategic intent or in drawing the value-map. Resources supplied by players may be employed in linked activities along one business process dimension or scattered among separate activities across multiple processes. Players usually exert sufficient influence to demand and receive slightly more than their fair portion of the surplus value created by the lattice, to earn an extra profit, as it were, on its investment.

> *Player:* orchestrates lattice operations and supplies resources for linked activities.

A *member* typically contributes limited resources and one or two activities in a lattice. Because their role is limited in scope and they are able to exert little influence, members must manage relationships creatively if they are to share in the real surplus—the value over and above that earned by being a regular supplier.

> *Member:* seldom performs more than one value-adding activity and does not supply managers to the core team.

It is possible for a company to be an initiator in one lattice, a player in another, and a member in yet another. British Petroleum (BP) may become the initiator of an oil-field development group by contributing 60 or 70 percent of the resources used. But it could also supply just its engineering expertise and assume a member's role. Or it could become a player by adding logistical support or procurement to its engineering services. (Meanwhile, in the gasoline market, it is a supplier lying outside its customers' lattices.)

The new economics of a networked world challenge management to maximize their companies' ability to capitalize on waves of innovation. Because single innovation is likely to be short-lived, sustainable advantage derives from continuous innovation based on a standard-setting, market competence (for example, drug discovery in pharmaceuticals). This turns old maxims of strategy formulation and execution on their head. Superior returns accrue to building low, dynamic, and even permeable barriers—partitions flexible enough to leak sufficient value to entice followers, but not so flexible to attract competitors capable of creating a new, market standard. Breakthroughs become chances to reinforce existing advantage.

points to remember

- **The core of an organization, its administrative structure, is also its source of inflexibility and high cost.**
- **A global lattice links independent units for specific purposes.**

In one version of the lattice, specialized units operate in one dimension (such as, product function or geography) for maximum efficiency, coordinated by a flexible top management team that customizes its involvement for particular purposes.

The lattice permits considerable delegation from the center to company units, however organized (whether by function, product, or geography), without loss of responsibility to the corporate center.

- The major corporation in the next decade will spread risk and reduce its required capital base by choosing key value positions in different geographic and product/service markets and outsourcing everything else, either formally to subcontractors or informally to other firms in the business lattice. The lattice reduces the complexity of managing businesses in global context.

- A firm usually plays one of three major roles in a lattice:

  The *initiator* supports lattice activities with strategic insight or the bulk of resources, or both.

  A *player* contributes significant resources, but typically does not participate in formulating strategic intent or drawing the value-map.

  A *member* contributes limited resources and performs just one or two lattice activities.

CHAPTER 5

configuring
the lattice

A LATTICE DERIVES ITS PARTICULAR FLEXIBILITY FROM
critical elements that are largely invisible. For example, it
is supported not by hardware, but by a pervasively distributed information system that generates value from
software that facilitates rapid knowledge exchange. A
lattice, moreover, transcends company boundaries to foster sharing resources with partners in alliances and outsourcing arrangements through well-defined business
processes, performance measurement, and market metrics. It's the device by which the e-Leader mobilizes
human beings to seize business opportunities.

Thus, organization charts make little sense for lattices.
More useful and instructive are tables of organization (that
is, listings of units) and configuration diagrams (that depict
active information or business process flows). Illustrations
such as that developed by BP showcase lattice elements and
their relationships, eschewing the formality of reporting

relationships. Indeed, charts that depict reporting relationships misconstrue the very essence of the lattice.

positioning a lattice in an industry

It is the industry value-chain that provides the basic economic rationale for the composition of a lattice. A management team can create for a given industry a "blueprint" of a lattice by analyzing the value-chain and defining the essential activities therein. It is a short distance from activities definition to required resources and capabilities to a lattice configuration diagram. Hence, modern executives often define the industries in which they are active much as they define their basic businesses. But look for that industry, whatever it is, to be redefined when a new or particularly exciting combination of resources and capabilities debuts as a value-creating lattice.

inside the lattice

The lattice is a fundamentally broad notion. "Local" lattices, although possible, cannot exploit the full value potential inherent in the concept. It is when multinational companies operating globally coalesce in a lattice that its true potential is revealed.

diagramming a lattice

It is possible to depict the principles of a lattice diagrammatically. The first principle is that of *porosity* (permeable boundaries). Whereas most executives still think in terms of organizing their companies to *do things,* in today's global business environment companies are increasingly a locus for identifying and assembling resources irrespective of where and whose they are. The lattice is the structure whereby disparate resources are directed towards a coherent end. Porosity refers to the flexibility that enables alliances, outsourcing, and rapid reconfiguration in the face of changing competitive circumstances. The temptation to concentrate on what is fully controlled, that is, on the company itself, must be resisted and executives should pay much greater attention to the complex relationships with other entities that constitute a lattice.

Implicit in porosity is that no activity in a lattice is immune from reassignment; no task is "reserved" to those currently engaged in it. If management concludes, by comparative cost analysis, that greater economic value will result from reassigning an activity and those who perform it, the switch will be made.

Porosity is driven by the fundamental logic of economic value creation. In some ways it is an oxymoron that business is about value creation; business has always been about making a profit. But, towards that end, business has also been about maintaining control over the assets processes, and people to its operations. Many managers admit, in confidence, to the marginally profitable assets their companies own and activities they perform—not to make money— but to ensure profitability.

When a lattice is used to create value, an execution is best advised to opt for the most efficient and capable units to include, regardless of their inclusion or not in his or her own company, and regardless of his or her degree of direct control over them.

The second principle of the lattice is reliance on *business process* and *activity* over function and division. Business process and activity are the building blocks of lattices. In practical terms, a business designer identifies first the broad business objectives to be achieved, usually the creation of products or services that generate profits, and then the business processes, such as product development, and logistics, brand management, that must be orchestrated to realize them. Each of these business processes is a broad work flow that can be subdivided into a subset of specific value-adding activities. The latter are constituted in such a way that:

- **They are relatively self-contained, with discrete inputs and outputs that can be obtained from others in the broader marketplace.**

- **They can be collectively benchmarked, that is, measured against equivalents elsewhere.**

- **A largely self-governing team can be assigned to perform the required tasks.**

This two-phase program—finding business processes and subdividing them into relatively self-contained activities— yields the internal construction of a lattice such as that depicted in Figure 5-1.

It becomes comparatively easy to direct the efforts of teams, departments, or other units and measure the results when the value-adding activities in a lattice are aligned along business process chains because each has a clearly defined

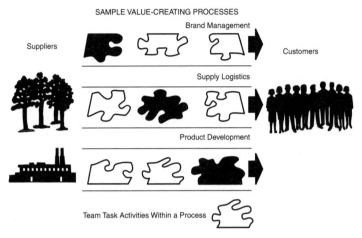

Figure 5-1 The Horizontal Process/Activity Focus of the Lattice

provider of inputs (look to the left in Figure 5-1) and buyer of outputs (look to the right in Figure 5-1). Each team can thus be given the basic mission of satisfying a buyer and subjected to the same constraint of doing so efficiently. With inputs, outputs, and activities clearly defined, economic value criteria can be used to measure each unit's degree of mission success. The connection between buyer and supplier being immediate, unhappy buyers can look elsewhere and, because of porosity—which grants them the freedom to reach outside the lattice—get what they need. Finally, because units become semiautonomous, central management need not waste time becoming aware of problems before a unit acts.

The third principle of the lattice, its *networked* nature, comprises two subelements: the networking of management and the networking of activity units. Although they intersect, these elements are sufficiently independent of one another to warrant separate discussions. It's important to recognize at this stage of presentation of the lattice that it will include elements from more than one company, which will be illustrated in Figure 5-5. Reference to units in the lattice are made from only one company as will be shown in Figure 5-3.

Achieving responsiveness on a global scale, management's fundamental role in a company must be rethought. Active managerial intervention in the internal activities of self-contained, mission-driven, customer-oriented activity units is not necessarily beneficial, indeed, may be disruptive and, therefore, costly. This is not to say that managerial hierarchy has no contribution to make to a lattice. Far from it. Hierarchy has a vital role to play in overall direction and coordination and the selection of business processes and unit leaders.

A company achieves a global mindset when its top executives make essential investment decisions, define missions, conduct economic value measurement, supply vision and leadership, and cultivate a culture and values that support effective participation in a lattice (see the left side of Figure 5-2) associated with this superstructure. The management information system interconnects the information systems of participating units, external to as well as within the company in order that operating data and policy directives can flow freely.

A *broader* "information substructure" (see the right side of Figure 5-2) enables activity teams to exchange information. Management's role in enabling and maintaining this system is vital, specifically with respect to ensuring that the often disparate participating units share (or learn) a common set of

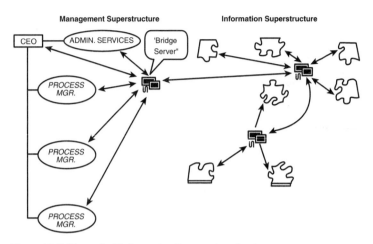

Figure 5-2 Networked Information Systems in a Lattice

values and terms that serve as a basis for communicating. Dysfunction in globally distributed lattices can often be traced to a failure to address the soft, or global, mindset associated with lattices.

The fourth principle of a lattice, *decentralization* is enabled by self-contained activity teams, the logic of horizontal business process work flows in which activity teams are rooted, and the distributed information system. In practical terms there is little to stop an activity team from spreading itself around the globe to find the unique sources of knowledge, assets, or other resources required to deliver economic value to its buyer. In fact, the logic of globalism, in which markets converge around common cultures and product, pushes management to seek competitive advantage through geographic dispersion. The lattice merely facilitates that dispersion.

The flags of particular nations that accompany the activities depicted in the business process chains illustrated in Figure 5-3 indicate where the "hubs" of these activities might currently be located ("currently" because there is nothing in principle to stop management or an activity team from moving its hub in pursuit of greater value).

Alliance capability, the last basic principle of the lattice, derives from porosity and the logic of economic value creation. The concepts of core competence and strategic focus suggest that owning all value-adding activities is highly wasteful of company resources; no single entity is likely to possess sufficient knowledge and skill to do *everything* required to compete in a particular industry value-chain at a consistently high level of performance. As long as this remains true, it

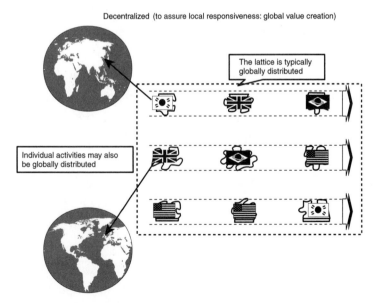

Figure 5-3 The Potential for Global Scope

will make economic sense for companies with complementary resources and efficiencies to collaborate.

Economic gains from outsourcing cannot be realized, however, if companies maintain self-contained structures. It is easy to see how traditional thinking inclines managers towards value-subtracting allocation capital decisions. A key activity cannot be abandoned just because it fails to generate value on the grounds that its absence might shut down profitable activities. Only if a company can ensure that another company will perform an activity well can it risk loss of direct control.

How can a company ensure that a prospective partner will honor its commitment? Writing complex agreements that incorporate explicit nonperformance penalties tends to eat up potential gains in transaction costs. Alternatively, one partner might become a subsidiary of the other. A contract, moreover, might not offer enough control for a tradition-bound management team. An arrangement that entails surrendering ownership and, therewith, control is resisted by many firms. The business alliance has emerged as a vehicle for bridging this gap. Thus, the lattice is alliance-capable as illustrated in Figure 5-4.

Alliance capability is the sharing by management of control over elements of a lattice that involve management teams of other organizations that are performing specialized tasks. Figure 5-5 illustrates in greater detail the connection between the core company and its alliance partners depicted by partners, the two arrows in Figure 5-4. Figure 5-5 is more complex than Figure 5-6 which will depict the entire lattice, because the connections between the elements of two companies (labeled A and B) are necessarily

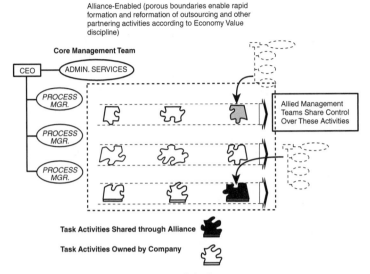

Figure 5-4 The Alliance Component of the Lattice

complicated by the fact that both are operating within lattice configurations.

Figure 5-6 brings the preceding five figures together. (Some elements in each have been dropped for clarity.)

The key characteristics of the lattice are as follows:

- Process-driven (sustain customer focus; maintain team disciplines; deliver/measure value-added)

- Decentralized (ensure local responsiveness; achieve global value-creation)

- Networked (truncate central hierarchy at the activity level to foster empowerment and sustain responsiveness; install information system and cultivate mindset to generate broad-based knowledge exchange)

- Alliance-enabled (introduce porous boundaries to enable rapid formation and reformation of "partnering" alliances

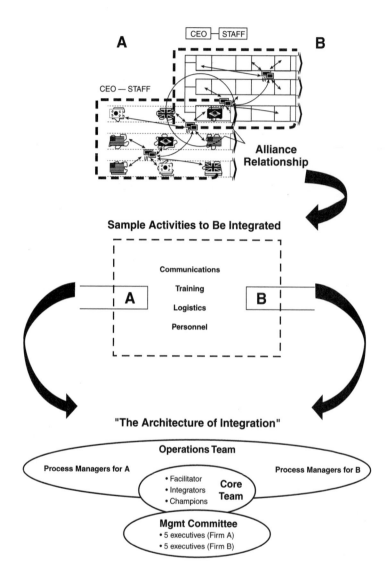

Figure 5-5 Alliance Architecture for a Lattice

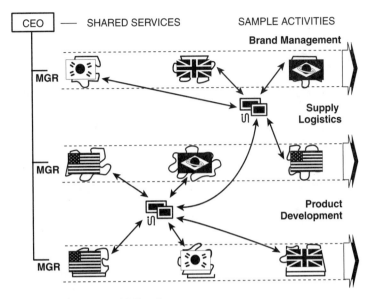

Figure 5-6 Bringing It All Together

according to shifting perceptions of where economic value is created)

from pyramid to lattice

Figure 5-7 illustrates the transformation from hierarchy to network enabled by the new design parameters that disperse authority outward from the center and downward from the top.

Figure 5-8 represents the dissolution of process-based into alliance-capable and, hence, lattice-compatible organizations as managers learn to disaggregate processes, identify value-adding activities within them, apply economic

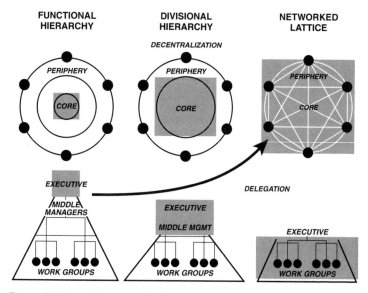

Figure 5-7 From Pyramid to Lattice

value analysis to determine which they should perform and for those they should not, and establish relationships with suitable alliance partners.

Table 5-1 summarizes the differences among pyramid, matrix, and lattice.

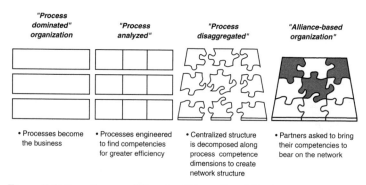

Figure 5-8 From Processed-Based to Alliance-Based Thinking

Table 5-1 The Pyramid, Matrix, and Lattice

	PYRAMID	MATRIX	LATTICE
WHY DEVELOPED	To coordinate many people with limited expertise in pursuit of a single objective	To integrate dual objectives (business and technical) into a single project	To ensure flexibility, simplicity, and lower costs than earlier approaches could deliver
Management Levels	Many	Several	Few
Span of Control	Limited (5-10)	Partial authority	Very broad (50+)
Reporting Relationships	To single supervisor	Split between at least two supervisors	Direct reporting relationships without close supervision; semiautonomous teams and self-leading individuals
Communications	Guarded data flows on a "need to know" basis	Limited; focus is on data needed to resolve conflict	Open; connectivity permits people to search out relevant data
Performance Appraisal	Supervisor	Project and function	Peers, customers, and team
Focus of Management	Coordination/ control	Cooperation/ negotiation	Collaboration/ flexibility
Decision-making	Issues referred up chain of command so long as each higher level will accept them	Issues referred to function/project interface; unresolved issues pass to top management	Issues expected to be resolved by those closest to them
Leadership	Boss/bosses appoint leaders	Project and functional managers appoint jointly	Leadership rotates within work teams
Goal-setting	By managers for direct reports	Established at level above function/project interface	Largely self-established within a framework established by higher executives

managing a lattice: the control tightrope

It might come as a surprise that CEOs are capable of exerting more power in lattices than in traditional, hierarchical organizations. In the latter, myriad reporting layers dilute the influence of their authority. But in the information-rich environment of the lattice structure, with its interconnected and integrated information systems, CEOs can effectively run organizations much vaster than their own companies.

Although access to an extensive web of information affords top executives the ability to operate to a great degree by remote control, they make a serious error if they succumb to the temptation to do so. Chief executives need to strike the delicate balance between keeping control sufficiently tight to keep people moving in the right direction and sufficiently loose to keep them motivated. Achieving this balance isn't about redrawing organization charts; it's about establishing mindset and creating values, about ensuring that people are committed to their jobs even when no one is watching them.

In the face of the temptation to overcontrol, a commitment to delegation is all the more important. Overcontrol dissipates the human energy that makes businesses successful. This can happen when managers operate by policy and control—people wait for direction from superiors instead of exercising initiative. Promoting initiative is the rationale for work practices such as teams, delegation, and empowerment. But deployed within organizations these practices were less valuable in themselves than as an antidote to the excessive control fostered by hierarchical organizations.

The irony of the CEO's position is that the lattice structure that more fully empowers top executives is eminently less enforceable than the hierarchical organization. Because the psychology of today's knowledge worker is different from that of traditional employees, managers cannot order the implementation of a lattice; it is a form that must be evolved collaboratively.

the challenge for top management

Jack Welch once defined his role as CEO of General Electric as having three key elements:

- **Allocate capital (that is, determine which investments to make);**
- **select people ("the winning play every time is the right person in the job"); and**
- **promote a culture in which GE executives from different businesses share the best techniques of management.**[1]

Welch's approach proved a magnificent value-creator, but it is already becoming outdated and is, in fact, somewhat old-fashioned. The significance of these elements persists, but each is transformed as a lattice takes shape.

Whereas Welch determined which investments to make, the twenty-first–century CEO rethinks the company's value positions. Twenty-first–century CEOs reconfigure the business lattices in which their firms participate. Whereas Welch promoted technique sharing, twenty-first–century CEOs animate lattices by facilitating knowledge exchange and promoting a mindset that exploits it.

Welch may well go down in business history as the last, and perhaps most effective, of the great chief executives of the business organizations that will, from the perspective of the future, be seen as creatures of the twentieth century. The latticed enterprise requires leadership (but no CEO). This is the real significance of the sudden emergence of great enterprises (Citibank-Travelers, Chase Bank) in which the top position, is, at least for a while, uncertainly defined.

The key new reality is that business lattices are broader than individual companies. A given CEO might "own" some elements in a lattice, "borrowing" others from vendors, and "sharing" still others with alliance partners. Hence, the lattice is not an organization as such entities are usually described.

A given CEO might help to establish a lattice, but does not manage it. The CEO sees customers, for example, as a representative of the lattice, not as the head of a company. What is important in a lattice happens *between,* not *within* individual centers of management. The lattice is organized and assembles capabilities, which it directs collaboratively and diplomatically with the fewest possible layers of formal control.

points to remember

1. The e-Leader reaches for the four dimensions of the lattice:
   - the value proposition or opportunity it addresses
   - the resources committed to it

- the linkages between its elements
- the guidelines by which it operates

2. There is little need to mention structure in connection with a lattice; a lattice's success is determined not by structure, but by business process management. Hence, there is no need for an organization chart; a chart is static, reality dynamic.

3. A lattice's success depends on the commitment and behavior of its people and participants; it draws as much from a culture that fosters a desire to play this game as from the formal authority associated with a position in it. It is given life—energized—by incentives and meaningful access to information:

   - Many firms today try to operate globally by utilizing a three-way matrix that reflects the necessary elements of the business: products (or services); functions; and geographic units.

   - Unfortunately, its many limitations and problems make the matrix difficult to manage.

   - Rearranging business elements into a lattice provides flexibility, reduces administrative complexity, and enhances the ability to focus on business globally.

powering via a
global mindset

The e-Leader finds opportunities and protects his or her market position via a continual scanning of business around the globe. The key to doing this well is to install a global mindset in the organization.

CHAPTER 6

mindset powers the corporate culture

TODAY'S E-LEADER IS AT HOME WITH A WORLD ECONOMY. He or she positions the company to find opportunities in the world as a whole, and to detect competitive threats. A firm misses opportunities without a truly global perspective and is vulnerable to competition. The power of a corporate culture comes from context it creates to direct the synergy generated by the interaction of people in the firm.

A global mindset provides management with the simultaneous local and global focus that is needed to make the best operational, resource, and strategic worldwide decisions. It is a combination of universal and parochial ways of looking at the world. Its purpose is to avoid what the Germans call *Ubersicht*—to see the details, but miss the whole.

A global mindset is a corporate culture that supports a company's simultaneous pursuit of its purpose and potential unrestrained by national boundaries, cultures, or languages, though these persist. A company with a global mindset can see both the whole (one world without borders, one market with six-plus billion potential employees or customers) and the parts (nations, regions, and continents; individual market segments).

A global mindset thus:

- **simultaneously assimilates parochial and universal points of view; and**

- **explicitly balances the tension inherent in these divergent perspectives.**

At the executive level, a global mindset is a window into the virtual value space that enables management to maneuver the firm within the business lattice so as to create and seize more value than could a firm conventionally situated. This can be done again and again by shifting and reconfiguring resources and capabilities.

Global mindset, though not the sole key to success in the global economy, is one of the most significant. It is crucial to the success of a global network, which like other organizational designs, relies on the commitment of those who compromise it.

The behavior of employees (management included), suppliers, and customers often belies the existence of a global network. A global mindset is the perceptual integrator that makes these constituencies universally aware that they are part of a geographically dispersed, but information-intensive environment that supports the rapid accumulation and suffusion of vast stores of knowledge of use in crafting strategies of arbitrage, synergy, and hedging.

It is implicit in a global network that firms relate their cultures to value creation, not, as is so often urged upon executives, to specific elements of their environment. There is a good reason not to relate the culture to anything but performance, since a consequence of organization design being perceived to be unrelated to performance is that it is thereby left to internal power politics to work out. In contrast, global mindset is a performance-oriented culture: it's opportunity- and synergy-seeking on a global scale.

How does a company develop a global mindset? It looks to the human components of the global network, specifically:

- **decisions, information flows, or actions that command management attention**
- **the language of communication (for example, values, references, definitions, symbols)**
- **behaviors and norms**
- **explicit and implicit incentives and measures**

balanced attention

A company that emphasizes only parochial concerns will miss broad, cross-market opportunities; a company that focuses exclusively on universal concerns will miss narrow, in-market opportunities. A global mindset requires balanced attention. Management must embrace the wide and narrow, the local and global perspectives, to achieve it.

Management can take specific actions to balance attention. To instill universal perspective, it can consolidate activities that seem to be replicated across geographic zones; for example, by establishing global brand management. To instill parochial perspective it can empower localized, if divergent practices among activity teams (that is, integrate, not homogenize). Finally, it can use the levers of resource allocation and performance management to promote balanced perspectives among lattice participants, to keep everyone thinking universally about what they see even though their immediate scope for action might remain local.

A global mindset is nourished by the free flow of ideas. This is facilitated when lattice participants share a common language—a Latin, so to speak—in which to express and exchange ideas. Such a language will emerge on its own— vocabulary will be acquired and shared metaphors emerge as a consequence of interaction; but speeding its evolution, particularly if lattice participants are many and varied, will see its value-creating potential realized sooner. A company that seizes the challenge and acts can:

1. **Hire skilled facilitators to help surface less obvious differences in how those with divergent backgrounds perceive similar phenomena.**

2. **Provide ample opportunities, perhaps in parallel with knowledge exchange platforms, for team representatives to work on language.**

behaviors and norms

Activity teams must willingly feed their ideas into and be receptive to others' ideas delivered via a lattice's knowledge-exchange engines. If team members are locked into behaviors or norms that preclude idea sharing, a lattice will tilt towards a local perspective.

A company can take three actions to instill appropriate behaviors and norms: (1) It can establish recruiting parameters, including realistic job previewing (RJP), that help it screen out people who are not sufficiently flexible to exchange ideas of their own volition. (2) It can give visibility to role models, managers, and others drawn from across the lattice who are committed to a flexible style of working. (3) It can attempt to instill the desired behaviors through training.

incentives and measures

A global mindset is ultimately reinforced or destroyed by the incentives and measures that operate in a firm's global network. Implicit (and, hence, invisible) are often more compelling than explicit incentives, but both must be aligned with performance measures. Rewarding individuals for sharing ideas will, for example, not be effective if individual contribution to success is measured.

A company can take three actions to ensure that incentives and measures are appropriate and aligned. First, it must ensure that it understands all of the incentives at work in the lattice. To achieve the stated strategic intent should be the ultimate focus of every person in a lattice and any cross-cultural dynamics that divert team members from this purpose should be identified and purged. Second, individual performance measures must be made consistent with a team environment. Only when team members' contributions to others' successes are rewarded on a par with contributions to their own successes will they willingly share their best ideas with others. Third, it must acknowledge that there are many ways to achieve success in an empowered team environment. Measuring output rather than effort is one way to send this message.

operative characteristics

A company with a global mindset is better able to identify plausible alternative scenarios, assess what-ifs, and reconfigure the global network to accommodate prevailing conditions because it views holistically the tasks at hand and the resources that can be brought to bear on them. A fundamental characteristic is that it substitutes a value-seeking orientation for a focus on authority structure, reporting relationships, or any other element of conventional organization. Inasmuch as it is about orchestrating the activities of many diverse, and often only loosely connected individuals, it is partly motivational. A key dimension is attention, which a global mindset directs to geography, business unit systems, common or shared facilities, corporate performance measurement, nontraditional organization, and innovation.

A global mindset prepares a company to grapple with being raised by the world economy, among them: Which countries should I enter and how? What should I do locally, regionally, globally? We're involved in a major global project;

what should we be cautious about? Can we better design our engagements? Are the new math and chaos theory relevant and, if so, how might they be applied? If we have many plants, should we have fewer; if few, more; and where should they be located?

Global reach is essential to economic growth and fiscal responsibility, localism to community, efficiency, and sense of belonging.

It is anachronistic for a firm to speak of a "home" country or of "foreign" operations; the global firm is a disaggregated entity to which the world is home.

A global mindset is a product of the step-by-step integration of strategy and execution, specific strategic and organizational concepts. It enables management to "shape the game" by choosing a set of opportunities around the world, assembling lattices of resources with which to play each round, and deploying them.

geographic dispersion is not globalization

Being global in the new century will be less a matter of where a firm is situated than of taking the entire globe into account in deciding where to perform specific activities at a given time. In the extreme, a firm might search the globe and find but a single country in which to operate and still, in a real sense, be a global firm even though it neither produces nor sells anything outside of that country. This is, of course, an unlikely scenario; a firm of even modest size is likely to find customers or suppliers outside its country of origin if it looks carefully, and looking carefully is a central tenet of globalization. Contrarily, a company might have subsidiaries the world over and yet not be global because each operates in one country without reference to any other. Such a firm would be a holding company of many geographically isolated firms.

Globalization is *how,* not *where,* a company does business. Global is a geographic term; what most people understand globalization to mean is that a firm operates all over the world. In fact, it means something quite different.

As used to describe an economic process, globalization refers to the internationalization of markets, not firms. In an international market some firms operate in many countries, some in but a few, but enough operate outside their countries of origin that it is the markets, not the firms, that have become globalized. At the level of firms, globalization refers to encounters between and interactions among business units irrespective of their geographic locations.

It is thus less a matter of geographic dispersion of sales or sourcing than it is a mindset, a disciplined habit of searching the globe for the most advantageous places to do business and seizing whatever opportunities are revealed.

In a most important development with respect to global firms, products and services that originate in one country achieve greater popularity in others. For example, Eli Lilly's new schizophrenia drug, which has enjoyed its greatest sales in the United States, was developed elsewhere.

Clearly, there are many ways to be "global." A global mindset can lead firms into many different relationships to geography. In light of the many studies of globalization that emphasize—and managers' loose application of the term to mean—geographic dispersion of firms' activities, it is neither possible nor wise to try to divorce the term from geography. But its related and more important meaning—the one that references not firm geography, but firm psychology—should not be lost. Globalization turns on the question of whether a firm has a global mindset.

A growing number of firms are multiplying activities around the world without a valid business justification, a counterproductive practice appropriately termed *mindless globalization*. On the evidence of other companies for which growth has trailed off, many top executives look abroad for growth opportunities. But when the CEO says, "We're doing global product mandating and now have a global supply chain," many business unit managers respond, "Yes, but it's inefficient and I want flexibility." For the business unit manager cognizant that products designed for the conditions of one nation may not work in another, that sales to particular countries may require greater customization than global product mandates permit, and that supplies obtained in some countries may not meet specifications for products produced elsewhere, globalization as driven from headquarters is merely a slogan, divorced from business needs.

The problem is the consequence of globalization being perceived as a geographic pursuit rather than a matter of mindset. Top executives with a global mindset want to be assured not that their business activities are scattered hither and yon over the globe, but that the best places in the world to make, sell, and buy are found and exploited.

Pursuing global product mandates, a well-known manufacturer of communications equipment marketed in China a product superior in functionality to, but much larger and heavier than, that of a competitor. That the competitor's product ran off with the market was due not to any lack of appreciation for quality on the part of the Chinese, but because local site managers lacked freight elevators to take heavy components to the top floors of buildings where they were to be installed. Local unit managers, although they had foreseen this difficulty, had been unable to resist edicts from the top to attempt to place the company's products in inappropriate markets. Key executives, convinced that they were globalizing, were, in fact, pursuing geographic dispersion.

A company wants to pursue geographic dispersion only when it makes economic sense. If careful examination reveals that limited geographic dispersion maximizes potential value creation, activities should be limited thereto. As circumstances change, so may the specifics of dispersion. Geographic dispersion pursued in this manner reflects a global mindset.

seeing opportunities in a global context

A company must view opportunities and risks in a global context to be successful in the global marketplace. It must therefore do more than merely operate in multiple countries; it must be at home in each. This is achieved by instilling a global mindset, which requires that management:

- Reshape the corporate culture to broaden and deepen its values;

- install new economic and social incentives and human resource policies that broaden employee and management horizons; and

- press executives to embrace a more "global" perspective in assessing risk and making asset allocation and other decisions.

The reasons for these changes are twofold:

- *Global activities require a global management style.* In a company in which asynchronous activity is the norm (that is, at any given time some parts of the firm, because it sprawls across 20 or more time zones, are sleeping), the central management structure cannot rely on "remote" controls from headquarters to stay on top of local operations. It must be able to delegate authority without inviting anarchy. Hence, headquarters can no longer be sole arbiter of policy, but must share responsibility widely with lower levels able and willing to accept it.

- *The value of a company is in its know-how, not in its what-do.* Value is embodied in the knowledge of products and making of markets, not in the making of products or knowledge of markets. One of the best ways to ensure that knowledge is used is to empower the front-line employees who are best positioned to capture and transmit it. To do this well they must possess knowledge about a wide range of possibilities in many countries—the global network—and be inclined to use it—the global mindset.

Developing a global mindset requires careful thinking about how to leverage intangible assets such as knowledge across cultural boundaries. Global companies must address the ambiguity that often accompanies greater diversity to ensure that employees drawn from a widening range of cultures and locations interact effectively. They must invest in the creation and maintenance of a common language and suitable infrastructure to facilitate communication; develop and reinforce a supportive culture; embrace multiple, cross-unit personnel assignments; and devise incentives that promote the capture and sharing of lessons learned.

A global mindset percolates down from top executives to all levels of an organization. Tendencies towards fragmentation can be countered by deploying reporting and control systems provided with financial (profit, cost) or operational (scrap rates, customer satisfaction indexes) metrics that deliver similar decision-making signals regardless of where the information is generated. Finally, being as often parochial as global, efforts must be made to ensure that top-level decisions reflect global as well as local priorities, as by installing standardized reporting systems that generate site-specific performance data that can be aggregated or compared across sites.

it takes a global leader

A company cannot embrace a global mindset until its executives do. Executives who believe, explicitly or implicitly, that their chapter is national will run their business in a national context and their company will remain national. Interestingly, this mental constraint afflicts even companies with highly successful nondomestic operations. It is as though executives of multinationals compartmentalize their mental maps of the world; they seem to believe that "multinational" confers the right to live in many different places and that "global" signifies "displaced persons" instead of "citizens of the world."

Executives intent on operating a truly global enterprise must be prepared to engage in new roles. They will no longer be issuing detailed orders and reviewing daily operating results. Instead, they will be adopting and instilling in their companies a global mindset. To this end, they will be setting direction; identifying and juggling assets—people, facilities, brands, and knowledge—to maximize value creation; choosing implementation vehicles ranging from alliance partners to internal competence building to mergers and acquisitions; and selecting, motivating, and appraising the teams assembled to execute their companies' stated goals.

The list of challenges to tomorrow's executives is somewhat different from that for firms, generally, and such challenges that are the same have different nuances. Figure 6-1 illustrates the "inside-out" nature of leadership in a global enterprise: from strategic intent, through mindset, to behavior as embodied in key operating mechanisms, namely, human resource policies (people), structure, information systems, and planning.

In a global enterprise, management provides strategic vision, direction, and purpose. To do so, it must investigate and forecast changes in environment, filter this data into planning frameworks, and test the appropriateness of conclusions for setting new direction.

Management also typically seeks to instill a particular set of behaviors in organization members. In a global enterprise,

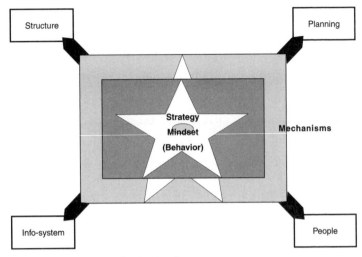

Figure 6-1 Tomorrow's Leadership Activities

key behaviors include: *cohesion*—a willingness to work with others across cultural boundaries; *initiative*—a willingness to take action in the absence of direction; *exchange*—a willingness to openly share ideas with and embrace ideas originated by others beyond the local work team; *stability*—a willingness to remain engaged in work even as it changes in response to new conditions; and *flexibility*—the willingness to adapt as conditions require.

Figure 6-1 illustrates how tomorrow's global management acts to make strategy and implementation one. It does so by intervening in the operation of the global enterprise through the following set of internal mechanisms:

- **Promulgation of vision and values.** This mechanism operates less through formal authority and direct orders and policies than through articulation of a clear vision, inculcation of appropriate and relevant values, active and thoughtful attention to, and reflection upon, the concerns of those being led.

- *Innovation (particularly in shaping and reshaping work processes)*. Key middle managers will become "process-owners" to ensure that design issues are dealt with by the organization's empowered teams.

- *Growth*. Management will continue to manage this key mechanism, principally through outsourcing deals, alliances, acquisitions, or divestitures that shuffle processes and nodes into and out of the network in line with economic value philosophy.

- *Discipline*. The nature of control, primarily with respect to the process-centered teams that do the work in a networked environment, will likely change, but the need for measurement and feedback will persist.

- *Coordination*. Even as management continues to support the information system and invest in building the global mindset required for coordination, employees will be asked to assume greater responsibility for making these mechanisms work in practice.

The foregoing management mechanisms and employee behaviors are embedded in a broader institutional architecture that comprises an information system, organization structure, and human resource policies. The management of global enterprise continues to shape vital elements of this architecture.

- *Information system*. This element of an organization's control system supports analysis of data that inform decision-making and provide the basis for implementation. One key innovation of a network structure is that it improves responsiveness by directing information to teams and management simultaneously.

- *Organization structures.* Management must define activities (such as products, markets, and projects), assign processes (not functions!), and determine levels of delegation and centralization to be established consistent with its view of what constitutes the appropriate degree of authority to be assigned to teams. A process-centered organization still requires an architect.

- *Human resource policies.* Management retains responsibility for selecting, placing, and rewarding (that is, motivating) people. It hires and fires, appraises, and rewards and punishes judiciously if it hopes to capture the full benefit of empowerment. It must pay particular attention to morale, an indicator of success in discharging its responsibilities, and to culture, a repository for values and other intangible motivators that exert considerable influence in the absence of direct supervision.

- *Planning.* To respond to continually changing opportunities and risks in the global marketplace planning will, of necessity, be done on a daily or weekly basis.

points to remember

The e-Leader recognizes that:

- A global firm is at home everywhere it does business.

- The most important aspect of globalization is not geography, but mindset—the search for opportunity on a worldwide basis.

- Implicit in global mindset is that management decisions take into account circumstances, opportunities, and risks across the globe.

- Absence of a global mindset in the field is a frequent source of conflict over corporate globalization initiatives.

- Absence of a global mindset at headquarters is a frequent source of lost opportunities and competitive setbacks in the field.

- A global mindset presumes that e-Leaders will:

  manage assets globally;

  build competencies globally; and

  create value globally.

- To sustain a global mindset e-Leaders must build into it:

  resource allocation;

  executive development; and

  performance management processes.

CHAPTER 7

being global

THE E-LEADER RECOGNIZES THAT BUSINESS IN TODAY'S HOT technology environment and global scope is very complex, and tries to simplify it to make execution of strategy more feasible. Global operations driven by global mindset are not elements of corporate structure, but rather reflect the relationship of a firm to geography. Such operations might be seen as a continuum of dispersion, with just one form of organization changing underneath the five forms described below.

These are not stages. They are presented sequentially to illustrate the steady progression of discretion outward from center. A company might be expected to proceed from the least to the most expensive form of internalization, and in the past this was often the case. With the advent of the Internet, however, a new company is as likely to find its first customers abroad as down the street.

When discussing globalization journeys later in this book, we will see companies choosing each of the five ways. Some choices were well made; some poorly.

There being no commonly accepted definitions for them, terms such as *multinational, transnational,* and *global* tend to be used interchangeably, which is unfortunate as there are significant differences. The following labels and definitions are applied with the purpose not of imposing terminology on readers, but of expressing and thinking clear.

In the paradox of global mindset and connectivity, world geography is no longer a key element of a global firm. It is mindset—a pervasive point of view that transcends location—that makes a firm global. A company in a connected world can be global without leaving its office by accessing the Internet.

The five forms of global organization described below do exhibit varying degrees of structures, but the home office/home country central point begins to look increasingly like a node in network. Global mindset is a continuum. As a firm globalizes, there develops some convergence in the diverse approaches of individual nodes in the network to how things are done. Parochialism is not extinguished by, but increasingly informs the emerging global perspective. If management is adept at inculcating mindset, it doesn't matter whether the firm's network comprises one node or 100 because the Internet takes the entire network to the world. All of which is to say there are not so many stages to becoming global as different ways in which it is advantageous to a firm to be global. What was sequential is now simultaneous.

Of the five general forms of global organization, only two are efficient: the exporter and the world enterprise. The inefficiency of the other three forms—international, multinational, and transnational—derives from their undue complexity and concomitant operational expense. Firms operating under these predecessor forms will necessarily—as they evolve a global mindset—transition to either an exporter or a worldwide enterprise. A global mindset effectively renders international, multinational, and transnational forms unstable.

exporters

An exporter sends products or services abroad from a home country. The company simply finds customers for its offerings outside its domestic market. This is an appropriate form of globalization when the domestic market is the best place in the world to produce. When it is not, better production sites abroad are ignored; the exporter is not global, but a myopic firm (see Figure 7-1). In an Internet world firms are

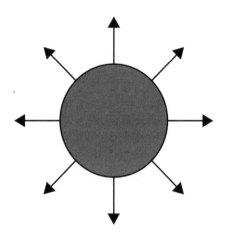

Figure 7-1 An Exporter

going to be called upon to export from their domestic platforms whether they want to or not—and whether or not
they are ready to do so! A firm with a de facto Internet presence offers its products or services to the world; as soon as it
begins to export, it has become global from an export plat-
form. In this sense, exporting is a reinvigorated form of
being global.

international companies

An international company clones specific functions in other
nations (usually initially sales, sometimes production as
well, as did Sony, for example, in an effort to establish itself
within the United States in anticipation of a feared round of
protectionism). (See Figure 7-2.) This form replicates the
home country company—without significant links among

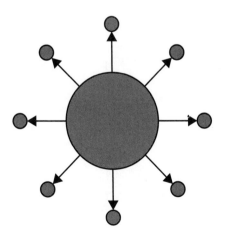

Figure 7-2 An International Firm

the various national companies, without cross fertilization of managerial approaches—with little or no local control, international companies generally being managed centrally and structured to facilitate this. Key examples are major Japanese companies that operate subsidiaries in other countries.

multinationals

Multinationals, too, clone their operations in many countries, but, unlike international companies, provide links among their national subsidiaries. Each subsidiary seems to have a local personality that includes host country management and two-way communication with the home country. Among the national subsidiaries, however, there is little

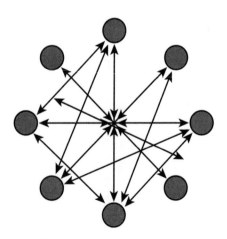

Figure 7-3 A Multinational Firm

communication. (There are exceptions: Nypro, a United States-based company that performs contract manufacturing for other companies, promotes communication among its national subsidiaries by having each report to a board that includes representatives for the others.)

Because it has been adopted by many prominent companies, including, for example, Ford, some observers see this as the emerging model. (See Figure 7-3.)

transnationals

A transnational company distributes specific competencies to different countries and manages business among the resulting national subsidiaries from its home country headquarters. (See Figure 7-4.)

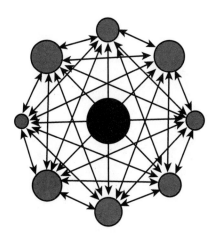

Figure 7-4 A Transnational Firm

world enterprises

The world enterprise, if it has an exclusive headquarters at all, does not view the country in which it is located as a home country. Its competencies, like those of multinationals, are dispersed around the world, but are viewed as nonnational. These entities do business with one another, often in a highly decentralized manner almost as if they constituted a free market internal to the company. (See Figure 7-5.)

Peter Drucker said of this form of organization: "There is only one economic unit, the world. Successful . . . companies," he added, "see themselves as separate, nonnational entities."[1]

A large, complex company (for example, General Electric) might have elements of each of these forms in its constituent parts or be in a state of transition from one form to

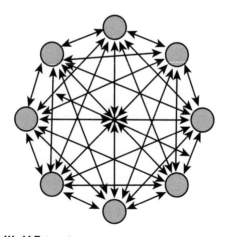

Figure 7-5 A World Enterprise

another (such as, Asea Brown Bovari). The News Corp is an example of a company that became transnational directly. It leapfrogged the exporter form and continents to build a global business through acquisitions. News Corp began to pursue acquisitions in Britain, jumped from Europe to America, and from there to the global marketplace. Little attention was paid to cost control and rationalization until near-bankruptcy in the early 1990s imposed greater discipline on the company.

News Corp's acquisitions strategy involved techniques developed in Australia for making profitable previously loss-incurring enterprises (such as *The Sun,* now the most profitable newspaper in the world). "If you're the producer of something, to guarantee your software gets to the public you need some distribution systems," explained Rupert Murdoch. "You can't own all the distribution, but if you control a lot of the distribution in Britain and in one of the countries in Asia, that's enough. That gives you leverage everywhere. I'll go global and try to use global leverage. That's my technique."[2]

Having built up its English language print-media franchise, News Corp turned its attention to television and film, targeting U.S. television stations and a U.K. satellite broadcast system. Building on its British base, News Corp began in the 1980s to seize opportunities in the United States to create new markets or run existing properties more profitably.

The company is run by a small corporate staff that relies on financial reports from its many subsidiaries, each of which is managed on a profit/loss basis.

In the early 1990s all three major markets in which News Corp operates were hit by recession simultaneously and the company had to renegotiate its credit arrangements to stave off bankruptcy. Geographic distribution, once perceived to be a hedge against the business cycle, provided no defense when Europe, America, and Australia declined simultaneously.

To protect itself in future from similar occurrences News Corp has created divisions for the purpose of clarifying operating relationships among its subsidiaries. It has also increased the size and complexity of its headquarters as necessary to manage its global media concern and established priorities for expansion. Finally, the combination of asset sales and debt and equity offerings undertaken to resolve its financial crisis has reduced the company's overall debt obligation and mitigated concerns about its financial future.

only two types really make sense

As emphasized earlier, only two of the five forms of global organization—exporter and world enterprise—have the staying power enabled by economic efficiency. The other three—so continually used by companies and so much studied by management theorists—are variations without economic justification.

Most firms evolve from exporters to world enterprises. An emerging global enterprise usually pursues three related aims with respect to its export markets: to find more such markets; to find more customers in each market it serves; and to find more efficient ways to expand its customer base. In the pursuit of more markets and more customers, a company typically progresses from reliance on remote-reach marketing tactics such as print and on-line catalogs to direct manufacturers' agents to company-employed traveling sales agents to local selling teams to, ultimately, local sales and marketing organizations. Upward trends in sales revenues justify committing greater overhead and supporting assets to nondomestic operations. The pursuit of more efficient ways to reach its customers typically leads a company to progressively internalize the logistical pipeline: from exporting existing products from existing domestic plants, through brokers, to eventually manufacturing and selling locally, through wholly-owned local supply chains, products tailored to local markets. Again, rising volumes trigger greater local presence.

Having deployed a host of local operations, perhaps in many markets, the management of a developing global enterprise finds itself addressing the fundamental issues of scale and duplication. Replicating the same activity across multiple markets is expensive and often counterproductive, but consolidating activities through global mandates can also be expensive when it hampers responsiveness or impairs local marketability. So management must ask itself at what points in the value-chain does it make sense to localize activity—explicitly accepting duplication as the price of effective responsiveness—and at what points does it make sense to globalize activity into geographically shared services—explicitly accepting the price of losing local responsiveness to gain global scale. This focus on getting the cost paradigm right might last for decades—as has been the case in the auto industry—or for but a very short period—as seems to have been the case among computer-chip manufacturers.

As a global enterprise matures, geographic distinctions fade; having evolved a global mindset, it is at home wherever it operates. It enters and exits key local markets around the globe, perhaps by establishing broad-based alliances that enable it to impose on the local community specific standards and practices for doing business—actively seeking to preempt the competitive options of others by leaving them no market space in which to learn and grow.

Why only two forms of organization are able to effectively navigate this evolution is illustrated in Figure 7-6. In essence, the exporter and world enterprise possess an

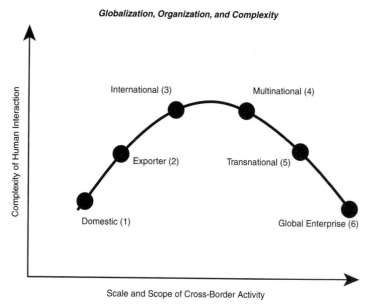

Globalization, Organization, and Complexity

International (3)   Multinational (4)

Complexity of Human Interaction

Exporter (2)   Transnational (5)

Domestic (1)   Global Enterprise (6)

Scale and Scope of Cross-Border Activity

Figure 7-6 Evolution of Forms

elegance of design that minimizes complex human interaction. Complexity in excess of what is needed to run a firm effectively adds to cost in a variety of ways. It incurs the expense of bureaucracy needed to coordinate, time lost in decision-making, and increased likelihood of errors.

Why do firms seek to be international, multinational, or transnational when these forms are inefficient? The answer is that they tend simply to evolve into these forms. Having no vision of the ultimate end of the evolution—the world enterprise—they are condemned to rediscover these intermediate forms and incur the costs of their inefficiencies. The evolution of forms is formalized in Figure 7-6.

- (1–2) Increasing scale and scope improve a domestic firm's profitability and lead to the perception of opportunities abroad. This pushes domestic companies into exporting and adding elements of value abroad.

- (2–3) Newly international firms encounter increasing complexity, which triggers increasing costs that reduce profitability even as scale increases.

- (3–4) As the company becomes multinational, the complexity of human interaction required to run it from a central point completely offsets gains to be had from further increases in scale, necessitating changes to its internal management systems.

- (4–5) A shifting mindset—whereby patterns of interaction are simplified and greater emphasis is placed on values, training, delegation, and decentralization—transforms a multinational into transnational organization.

- (5–6) The transnational evolves through further simplification into a more purely global enterprise. Globalization reduces cross-border differentiation, and connectivity reduces the time invested in cross-border communication, enabling existing management capacity to be stretched across more international operations and, thereby, continued growth in scale concomitant with a decline in complexity. As central control fades into a network of connections between local affiliates, members of the central management team become network controllers rather than command and control decision-makers. As national economies converge and differentials fade, the need for communication to manage them decreases and eventually disappears; the world form is, in essence, a domestic company on the global stage.

points to remember

The e-Leader recognizes that of the five principal forms of global organization:

- exporter,
- international,
- multinational,
- transnational, and
- world enterprise,

only two of the five types make sense:

- exporter, and
- world enterprise.

The great value of the Internet and electronic commerce is that it permits a firm to dispose of the three transitional forms and rely only on the two effective ones.

CHAPTER 8

energizing people

IT IS NOT ENOUGH FOR THE E-LEADER TO HAVE PEOPLE IN A firm to think globally nor even to have restructured organizationally to exploit global opportunities. People of divergent cultures, in asynchronous operations, and with varying institutional constitutions must be motivated to seize the opportunities that confront them, work in complex settings, and employ connectivity imaginatively. In short, a firm must energize its people to realize potential value.

Great administrators are of no use to firms as leaders unless they can energize others. This is true for all managers, not least those at the top of a firm's hierarchy.

How are people in firms to be energized so that they work at top performance and full advantage of advanced technology? Many manufacturing firms have achieved this by deploying empowered (or self-led) teams to meet overseas competition by improving productivity and quality simultaneously. Although it has been largely responsible for the resurgence of American competitiveness in manufacturing, this initiative has been poorly applied elsewhere. Our companies operate their factories with empowered teams and rely on old bureaucracy for almost everything else. It's time to take the notion of empowered teams out of the factories, adapt it to nonmanufacturing environments, and, ultimately, use it to animate entire organizations.

excitement in the workplace

To energize the people in a global firm, it is necessary to take into account the things that define who they are: gender, race, ancestry, culture, religion, institutional affiliations, and so forth. At a minimum, it is crucial that people's defining characteristics not be a basis for giving offense. Beyond this, all that might be required to energize them are traditional business motivations: income status, possessions, wealth. But it might also be possible to reach for stronger motivations, such as excitement about the work at hand (as in high tech and some professions) and contributions to a cause (such as the modernization of a country). Such motivations are often important and significant in the national subsidiaries of global firms.

Often in the hope of holding labor costs in check, managers and pundits have for years emphasized job satisfaction as an alternative source of motivation. But this is largely a mistaken notion.

European researchers have demonstrated in recent years that job satisfaction can as often undercut as supply motivation, as must be evident to anyone who thinks systematically about his or her own experience in the work place. "I've got the best job in the world; I have nothing to do and get paid well" is consummate job satisfaction, but hardly qualifies as motivation. Some of the hardest working, most motivated contributors, on the other hand, were found to be not at all satisfied with their jobs and even frustrated and upset by others who were not working so hard or by lack of imagination or commitment that undermined the success of the firm. This absence of job satisfaction can work on behalf of a company if it becomes a source of creative tension that helps to energize others.

The greatest contribution that job satisfaction can make is to forestall the kind of general dissatisfaction that gives rise to strikes or other broad disruptions. This is, of course, important. But generally the best that can be said for job satisfaction is that, when accompanied by positive motivation, it is a marvelous thing. But it does not motivate top performance.

If job satisfaction is not the motivator firms seek, what is? Experience in professional service firms and high-tech research and development has demonstrated that excitement is a major motivator. Excitement is job satisfaction in spades, or, rather, it is not job satisfaction at all. A person can be satisfied as was pointed out above, doing nothing. Excitement presupposes enthusiasm and involvement. A firm that aspires to top performance must get its people excited about their work.

This is difficult for managers, many of whom are not at all excited about the work they do. Too often managerial work is routine and administrative, instilling in managers an attitude of boredom rather than excitement and anticipation. Communicated to others, this attitude undermines performance.

the new global culture

A firm can create a global culture that transcends differences in national, ethnic, and religious cultures. It ought not to be, however, the home country culture exported. Rather, it should be an element of the evolving world culture.

culture as values

Culture is about values, not so much the values of a firm, an error of emphasis that executives often make, as of those within it. Executives who identify, codify, and promote the values of their firms forget that it is people, not companies, who do things. The values that matter most are those that are embraced by, and guide the actions of, the people in a firm.

To cultivate values is less a matter of codification and enunciation than of leadership and example. Executives, for example, often exhort their staffs to be more risk-taking only to have them gather outside at the break and say to one another, "Yeah, take a risk, and the first time something goes wrong, you're out of here!"

Those who advocate management by values, moreover, often seem to imply that executives can define and lead by, Pied Piper-like, a set of values to which all will willingly subscribe; but executives are not free of the societies in which they operate. In their home countries, leaders must adapt to national values; abroad, they cannot ignore local values.

To fashion and implement a unique set of values with real meaning is difficult. Recognizing that people who need to cooperate are often separated by a gulf of potential divergent interests and potential mistrust, the best one can do is try to identify and promote a set of values to which most of the organization seems willing to conform. Fortunately, there seems to be emerging in the world a set of values that can bind people together irrespective of nationality, gender, religion, race, and ethnicity. The best course of action for global firms is to focus on—that is, recognize, adopt, and lead in conformance with—this set of emerging values.

Key elements of this new set of values upon which networks of cooperation can be built include:

- **willingness to help others**
- **acceptance of personal responsibility for outcomes**
- **bias for action**

These three elements alone constitute the basis for an effective corporate culture for global firms. They do not conflict with the more sophisticated versions of most of the world's religions and cultures, nor are American values projected onto the global stage. They are a product, rather, of the confluence of European, African, Asian, and American (North and South) cultures.

These are also business values and broader in application. Willingness to help others is the basis for cooperation and partnerships, acceptance of personal responsibility for outcomes the basis for truly engaging in attempts to bring about meaningful change, and a bias for action the basis for moving beyond talk.

These values cannot simply be presumed. Is individual responsibility, for example, really an almost universal value? Are there not many cultures—African communities that believe "It takes a village" or people whose language does not include the word "I"—in which shared responsibility is the norm? Is bias towards action consistent with the Japanese value placed on lengthy consensus-building? Clearly, in different contexts specific values will have to be inculcated.

the challenge of cultural integration

Management has always established, maintained, and transformed culture, consciously or otherwise. Culture is simply the aggregate of shared values that enable employees with varied backgrounds, experience, and talents to work together towards common objectives. It has long been viewed as an important, albeit intangible, corporate asset, a potent motivator of productive (or disruptive) behavior.

Sustaining a suitable corporate culture is essential to a global enterprise that encounters multiple local cultures as it spreads around the world. A national enterprise's culture can usually build on a common history, educational and economic system, and language. A multinational company typically imposes a "culture of origin" on its local units, blindly accepting loss of integration into the local milieu as a cost of doing business. A world enterprise integrates the local culture it absorbs with the commonality it preserves into a seamless totality that supports the sharing of experience across all nodes. It is the porous boundary and interactive knowledge-exchange system implicit in the lattice structure that enables this cultural balancing act.

why less control is appropriate

Many managers believe that in the absence of directions and continuous performance-monitoring, organizations will decline into chaos. But where appropriate roles and incentives are in place, people tend to be self-organizing and self-starting. Absent the traditional executive-level command and control structure, and given appropriate parameters to guide behavior, patterns—not chaos—will emerge.

Ironically, many executives know this about markets, but don't believe it about organizations. That is, they acknowledge the so-called "invisible hand" that coordinates entire economies according to incentives that help markets to clear excess supply and demand and growth to occur, but are oblivious to the potential of this force in their own organizations, preferring to rely on a form of command and control that they would unilaterally reject in the large economy.

The global network organization thrives under the invisible hand, and languishes under command and control. It is a form that has been widely tested, notably in professional service firms, such as investment banks and heavy engineering and consulting firms, and in industries such as petroleum, electronics, computing, and the media.

hierarchy and empowerment

"Setting the tone" for organizations is a key role of executives. In large part, "tone" reflects the fundamental choice between a top-down directive and empowered-participative organization. Hierarchy satisfies the need for organizational decision-making and natural tendency of leadership to emerge among people in most settings; empowerment avoids crushing individual initiative. Debate over the relative effectiveness of these forms persists unnecessarily, as in the context of a firm they are complementary, not substitutable.

Firms need both. In a hierarchy, delegation is empowerment. In a flat organization, empowerment creates a hierarchy of leadership.

The price of excessive hierarchy is bureaucracy and inflexibility, of too little indecisiveness and, ultimately, anarchy. The issue is not hierarchy yes or no, but how much hierarchy and to what end?

conflict between headquarters and field

Corporate headquarters sometimes encounters resistance from business unit managers who, in light of rejection of overseas involvement, view home country globalization initiatives as inapplicable. If rejection is a consequence of careful consideration, it might be appropriate, but often business units simply do not actively consider worldwide possibilities in their business decisions. Myopia reigns and domestic or regional business is pursued as usual. Such instances are justification for corporate imposition of globalization initiatives over the resistance of business unit executives. Seeing the failure to identify opportunities on a global scale, corporate executives well might intrude with plans ill-suited to particular business units. Without careful *seeking* at the business level, however, no one knows what will work and what won't.

What is clear is that globalization initiatives in many firms are today imperfect at best. They are championed without clear understanding of whether or not they will be beneficial and rejected without clear knowledge of their potential value. Many top executives are consequently critical of their firms' failure to seize the full potential of globalization.

Globalization often underachieves its value-creation potential in part because firms fail to leverage existing assets effectively. A key underleveraged asset is personnel, a tangible entity that embodies intangibles such as knowledge, effort, initiative, and intelligence. To leverage its human assets, a firm needs a program of motivation that transforms individual elements (such as compensation, selection, and personal development) into a mutually supportive coherent whole.

regionalism is a cop-out

Many firms cope with the complexity of global activities by establishing regions. It would, however, seem that if a world enterprise is about exploiting differentials and synergies globally, then to stop at regionalism is to suboptimize. In fact, regionalism is in some ways the right way to go global. In principle, it makes sense to manage tangible assets on a regional basis, and intangible assets on a global basis.

This is the origin of much of the tension between headquarters and the field in many firms. The distinction between tangibles and intangibles is not made. Headquarters, which ought to be managing intangibles, tries to manage all assets; management of regional tangible assets inevitably embraces intangibles as well.

Consider the Walt Disney Company. Disneyland Paris's substantial tangible assets (its park, hotel, and so forth) should be managed locally, but its use of Disney's intangible assets (the company's brand name, in particular) must be managed globally. The essence of a global mindset is executives' and managers' ability to distinguish what should be done globally from what should be done locally and to manage the requisite coordination.

the challenges of cooperation

Because excessive central direction will destroy the complex mix of global and local initiative that is key to the success of a global enterprise, considerable authority must be delegated outward and coordination secured by the cooperation of all involved.

preconditions for cooperation

Cooperation becomes crucial when authority is shared with local business units and work performed by empowered teams. To ensure that cooperation occurs, management must establish a context that supports and facilitates it. The following set of preconditions will foster an environment that is hospitable to cooperation.

- *Goals not fragmented by function.* Management cannot expect people with a narrow view of work to understand broad goals. Marketing, finance, or personnel will not derive suitable meaning from a directive such as "run a process" because they cannot deliver on such a goal.

- *Sufficient competence at the local level to exercise delegated authority.* Management cannot expect people who lack ability or experience to act other than "blindly" in a given situation that might be worse than not acting at all. Only the competent should act.

- *Information required to support action available to those who have the option to take action.* Decisions should be made as close to the point of action as possible, provided that appropriate experience and supporting information are available.

- *Suitable measurements and rewards in place.* Measuring results, not actions, empowers people. Rewarding actions encourages reliance on procedures rather than action with an eye to achieving a specific result.

- *Fault-tolerant culture.* Successful delegation requires a clear, consistent set of circumstances under which mistakes will be tolerated. These rules establish what is known as the zone of delegation—a psychological space in which people can comfortably exercise delegated authority. Absence of tolerance for faults will inevitably be accompanied by absence of initiative.

fault tolerance

In latticed structure, process-centered teams are typically organized around generalized skills to ensure that employees will have the competence to understand broad goals and be able to assume some responsibility for managing "their" processes. A network structure's "open communications" enables teams to seek externally insight they might need but lack "on site" to solve problems. But a network neither naturally rewards results nor sets fault tolerance; these elements of culture and control lie outside the zone of empowerment. Cooperation cannot be effective so long as these elements remain under directive management.

There are four rules of thumb that managers can use to establish fault tolerance—to help them know when not to intervene in a unit's internal activities.

- *When a mistake is not part of a pattern.* Executives should intervene to encourage unit managers to share insights so that mistakes are not repeated. But they must also learn to let "first" mistakes go, provided that the following conditions are met. Why is this so important? Because taking initiative inevitably involves making mistakes. If mistakes are not permitted, initiative will not be taken.

- *When a mistake allows something new to be learned.* Companies must continually try new things to cope in an uncertain world. A mistake that teaches a company something new should be recognized as valuable and shared with others.

- *When a mistake is made in pursuit of an assigned goal and falls within assigned authority.* Delegation being a powerful grant of authority, top executives must encourage managers to stick to their goals. Mistakes that result from going *beyond* the scope of assigned authority are serious. But disappointment that occurs within the box must be considered only in the broader context of the results achieved at the end of the measurement period.

- *When a mistake is consistent with law and principles.* This condition is intended to preserve a company's values and to keep it out of legal trouble.

Fault tolerance is the source of the trust that enables self-leadership. As the level of trust rises, so does willingness to exercise delegated authority. Fault tolerance helps people understand under what conditions they should act; trust enables them to act.

points to remember

The e-Leader must energize the firm's people to realize potential value. To do this, he or she recognizes that:

- Job satisfaction is not much of a motivator; job excitement is.

- Firms should embrace an emerging global culture as a basis for engendering cooperation among workers of diverse nationalities, genders, faiths, and ethnic groups.

Initiative at the local level is facilitated when:

- Goals are not fragmented by function.

- There is sufficient competence at the local level to exercise delegated authority.

- The information required to support action is available to those who have the option to take action.

- Suitable measurements and rewards are in place.

- The company culture is fault tolerant.

A firm must be efficient and flexible to build value in a global economy.

Corporate executives believe that bureaucracy has been reduced and that greater efficiency has resulted; measurements tell a different story, namely, that there is still ample opportunity to reduce bureaucracy and increase efficiency.

Flexibility and efficiency are realized by delegating from the center and reducing bureaucratic roles of managers throughout an organization.

Firms reduce bureaucracy by:

- **reinvigorating the informal organization;**
- **selectively despecializing employees; and**
- **inverting the decision rule.**

speeding through decentralized planning

to be successful, a modern corporation must not only cultivate a global mindset and establish a global network, but also must be fast on its feet. In today's fast-moving, rapidly changing world, firms must migrate business strategy and planning out of the corporate office and into decentralized business units. The e-Leader must liberate planning from budgeting and make budgeting part of the business planning. The following chapters suggest a simple, three-step process that combines business strategy and execution at the business unit level in a fast, iterative process.

CHAPTER 9

three crucial steps

WITH STRUCTURAL BARRIERS TO COMPETITION FAST DISAP-
pearing as a consequence of electronic connectivity, market
deregulation, and improving technologies of many sorts,
how well and quickly a company reacts to change are all
that protect its positions. The e-Leader recognizes that fast
adaptability is the latest stage in the evolution of business
strategy. Initially, companies were urged to procure market
share, the data seeming to correlate it with profitability.
Then strategists dissected industry structure and urged
companies to seek strategic position, either by being low-
cost producers or by differentiating their products in such a
way that a price premium could be obtained. This was followed by exhortations to define core competencies and
strategic intent—this was strategy as stretch.

In today's fast-moving and unpredictable marketplace,
however, emphasis has shifted to speed—but not to chaos.

Those who heed the gurus who insist that chaos is a necessary accompaniment to speed are prey to confusion. A business is subject to disastrous mistakes in the absence of clear and logical direction. Chaos not only engenders confusion, it is not the right solution because it is subject to disastrous mistakes. What is needed is a disciplined process by which speed can be achieved quickly.

An e-Leader helps his or her firm to abandon the archaic separation of strategy and execution, of planning and implementation, and instead seeks to have it intertwine planning and execution in time as if in a double helix. The essential process for accomplishing this can be built around three steps: seeking, shaping, and securing. Generally, *seeking* is about discovering global opportunity; *shaping* is about locking in the opportunity; and *securing* is about seizing its value.

Seeking involves knowing where and what to look for. Shaping involves understanding how to extract value from global opportunities. Securing is the dynamic process of realizing that value. A firm that moves too fast will be consumed by innovation from which it will not derive full payoff; a firm that moves too slowly will be left behind. The dynamic process of seeking, shaping, and securing must appropriately be paced and executed in the correct sequence.

In Chapter 1 you read how Microsoft had entered one of a number of arrays being spawned by the microcomputer, then carved out of the large computer array a PC array, which it subsequently came to dominate. Recall that it was no less than IBM from which Microsoft spirited away the PC array and that it did so by recognizing that the value-map for the newer array was shifting to emphasize the operating system. What is most significant for our purposes here is how quickly Microsoft displaced IBM—in less than ten years.

That Microsoft did not do this alone is not only correct, but the whole point. By building value in cooperation with others in the context of a lattice, Microsoft was able to move much faster than it could have otherwise and, by actively shaping the lattice, was able to extract much more than what might have been expected to be its share of the value created. This classic example of the new strategy of speed applied in the context of business lattices is best understood in terms of the three steps of seeking, shaping, and securing.

No other firm will exactly emulate Microsoft. But although each firm's journey will be unique, the preferred sequence of steps will be common to all. A firm chooses a place to participate in the economic landscape, organizes (if it can) how the game is played, then seizes all the value it can. The journey of Sun Microsystems's Java product, although not the journey of Microsoft's operating system, nevertheless follows the three steps of the strategy of speed.[1]

In 1992 Sun found itself in a classic strategic market squeeze, the market for high-end workstations being eroded from below by sophisticated personal computers and from above by less expensive mainframes. While its strategy formulators were busy peering into the future, its strategy implementers were already hard at work on a possible solution and trying to "reinvent" the company along the way.

In January 1994 Sun was asked by a number of computer engineers based in Oslo, Norway to help build an unofficial Winter Olympics web site. Sun shipped a workstation and a

web site was born. The site, albeit simple, with event outcomes and low-quality photographs, was a hit. The Oslo
team had created one of the Internet's first sports web sites
and Sun's logo was on it, scooping IBM, an official Olympics
sponsor. Eventually IBM complained and Sun's logo was removed. But its web team had seen the site, made a copy for
Sun's own web site, and, via e-mail, invited the world to
visit. Many people did so.

When, in the wake of its Olympics coup, Sun's engineers
became intrigued with and began to explore the possibilities of the Internet, some company executives, concerned
that valuable work time was apparently being lost to net-
surfing, tried to impose an internal financial charge on time
spent on-line. Had the engineers acceded to management,
what was to become a marvelous opportunity might well
have been lost. But so strongly did Sun's engineers make the
case that the Internet was more than a playpen that management was forced to withdraw its proposal. When Sun executives subsequently took another look at the Internet, their
business sense was triggered—a network application might
just be the way out of the company's predicament. Making
Sun an Internet-focused company was the change in strategic direction that led to the Java application.

Nowhere in Sun's redefinition of strategy was there the
traditional separation of formulation and implementation.
The opportunity was recognized by the rank and file—
implementers, not formulators—and when the formulators
caught up, no one could plot an implementation sequence; it
had developed in the daily turmoil of the marketplace.

What had seemed chaotic to Sun executives was not
chaos at all; its strategy was simply not understood. In

fact, this is a useful definition of much of what is now described as chaos by management gurus: It is a system that is not yet understood. When Sun management, spurred by the stubborn resistance of the firm's engineers, grasped the significance of the Internet, the opportunity that opened up was the first step towards value creation. It had found a place in the business landscape among the lattice of firms working to build the general acceptance and utility of the Internet.

Sun's attempt to use its Java language to shape the future of the Internet and alter the value-map of the PC array—such that, according to the company's CEO, the network becomes the computer—mirrors Microsoft's earlier efforts to displace mighty IBM. Whether it succeeds will depend on the extent to which it can organize how the game is played, that is, how effectively it manipulates the lattices in which it is participating so as to maximize the value it is able to extract from the array.

Implicit in the new strategy of speed, as in so many innovations, is the discarding of current habits. Many companies' approach to business continues to reflect the ancient military model that treats strategy and its execution as separate activities, a legacy of a brief period during which large companies that commanded dominant market shares enjoyed the luxury of sufficient time and excess resources to invest in this artificial distinction. In strategy formulation according to the military model—a rigidly formal and hierarchical process—executives are the generals who plan; managers, the majors who assign; and employees, the soldiers who execute. Strategy is thus dictated on high, communicated down the ranks, and implemented at the bottom.

Because it so fully defines roles and responsibilities, it is a comfortable system for executives, management, and staff alike. But it is slow, rigid, often poorly informed, and crippling in today's fast-moving world. Firms plan things they can't execute and execute what they haven't planned.

What is needed is a system that can unite strategy formulation and execution, in a manner that is iterative and inclusive. In other words, it is continuous—not undertaken once to yield results that will be adjusted only at distant and discrete intervals—and brings the company's full experience base, not just the thinking of a few top executives, to bear.

What has evolved to satisfy this need is the three-step strategy of speed: *seeking* opportunities; *shaping* capabilities; and *securing* the potential. Used as a process, this strategy ensures that the changing potential of global business is explored and opportunities identified, assessed, and the most valuable targeted for action and resource allocation (*seeking*); that organizational capabilities are developed and strategic positions established (*shaping*); and that value is realized (*securing*). Seeking is a process of exploration, shaping of configuration, and securing of realization.

step 1: seeking

The world economy today is not only more complex, challenging, and risky than it has been, *but likely to become more so.* This is why exploring different directions of global development is so important.

The seeking step involves:

- **anticipating the geographical, industrial, and competitive "high grounds" that will enable an enterprise to capture value as the global landscape shifts;**

- **exploring trends in a changing world for value creation opportunities; and**

- **selecting the opportunities with the greatest potential for building value.**

Seeking is about anticipating the demands of twenty-first–century business. The companies that have made the most money in recent years are those that have anticipated the future—especially counterintuitive government or market movements—and positioned themselves to take advantage of resulting opportunities. For example, a hotel by Marriott opened in Warsaw a year or so before the fall of the Berlin Wall and claimed 120-percent occupancy for almost every night of the three years subsequent to that event. Similarly, modem manufacturer US Robotics, against the advice of many "experts" who believed that modems would be supplanted by satellite or cable-based communications, invested in new technologies and bought a number of competitor companies in the early 1990s. Internet use subsequently exploded, and US Robotics was better positioned than any other firm to sell modems to consumers and Internet service providers, ending up with almost 80-percent market share of a growing and highly profitable U.S. market.

Anticipating the future also means assessing nontraditional opportunities created by economic growth and restructuring. A smart player in a stodgy industry, Enron, for example, transformed a basic gas transmission business into an advanced financial derivatives business. Virgin Airways, in pitting itself against what was perhaps the stodgiest of competitors, British Airways, not only created a sense of fun in the air, but drove the larger firm to transform itself into a far more effective carrier. Denny's—one of many players in the U.S. fast-food business—by getting to Japan early, before most of its American rivals even considered leaving home, was able to establish what is now a dominant position (to the point of being considered a domestic company) in a market in which fast food was perceived to be something new.

step 2: shaping

To win big, a company must shape its chosen markets to suit its competitive strengths, in part, by tapping the potential of interconnectivity. This is done by creating self-serving boundaries around business opportunities. Historically, methods of creating boundaries—including ownership, lawsuits, patents, government regulation, and location—are fast disappearing as a consequence of market deregulation, variation in legal standards among nations, electronic interchanges, and technological advances in a growing number of industries.

Many newer methods of creating boundaries remain unfamiliar to today's executives. Consulting, for example, is an industry that lives within other industries in symbiotic relationships that are themselves barriers to competitors. Alternatively, alliances—especially with government and local institutions—afford companies access to value that would not otherwise be available to them. Competitors can also be kept at bay by tying up key suppliers or customers as alliance partners and by mounting one-to-one marketing initiatives that exploit information technology to support highly targeted sales and promotion efforts paired with customer retention and loyalty programs.

Successful barriers to new entrants and existing competitors are erected by leveraging key intangible assets—knowledge and brands—far more effectively than has likely been done in the past. Throughout the centuries value has largely been created by controlling and exploiting physical assets; for example, finding, mining, and marketing the world's minerals. In today's overexploited world, companies that are able to assemble, support, and maximize the effectiveness of global terms are better able to anticipate and react to changes in the ever more volatile international arena.

The primary strategic challenge to management in the twenty-first century will no longer be how to maximize the finite life spans of given technologies or innovations, but rather to learn to ride the waves of innovation that continually wash over and through the market space. Companies that do not learn to surf the continuous changes in technology will not survive long enough to need coherent strategies.

The new barriers to entry will be metaphysical, not physical, barriers in the mind, rather than statutory barriers such as preferred access to resources or state-sponsored protections, which will be auctioned off to the highest bidder and thereby become no barriers at all. The new barriers to entry will be attributes to flexibility, opportunity seeking, and speed of execution. Strategy will become a hunt for ideas, not niches, as transaction costs continue to fall and the sizes and shapes of companies shift in response.[2] Most strategists want the actors on the business stage to try to change the script; few see that today the other actors and the stage itself can also be managed.

Companies must prepare for the day when the advantage conferred by innovation fades, a day that will arrive when knowledge sharing is encouraged rather than discouraged. Instead of trying to ride the learning curve to a low-cost position or differentiating with special attributes, companies must attempt to make their products or services into market standard, then focus on the truly value-adding bits of the value-chain that form to fill resulting customer demand. Sustainable profits will be wrung out of setting standards for a web of value-adding suppliers rather than by preventing others from learning how to duplicate innovations. Companies that throw their doors open will fare better than those that hoard their secrets. Consider the example of Apple Computer.

For Dan Eilers, CEO of CIDCO, a Morgan Hill-based maker of Internet-enabled telephones, Apple's most instructive failure was its inability to capitalize on a ten-year technological lead once enjoyed by Macintosh computer. "The best technology does not always win," said Eilers. "The partnerships and the business model matter as much or more than having the best product." Eilers noted that the Macintosh remains a force in the publishing industry because Apple forged strong partnerships with graphics software makers like Adobe, Aldus, and Quark. But, Eilers pointed out, Apple didn't broaden the Mac's appeal by licensing the operating system to clone-makers or allowing it to run on Intel micro-processors.[3]

The walls and moats erected and sunk around today's companies will have to be leveled and filled. Companies will find it most productive to encourage discontented employees with new ideas for employing corporate technology to leave and found companies that proliferate the underlying technology standard. This can be done by offering them help in the form of capital and counsel. Nor will wise companies invest in every competency, function, and activity related to their business. Rather, they will limit investment to the portions that can generate superior returns, willingly partner with companies to create new sources of value, and solicit the help of the state to dismantle barriers erected by others that prevent the worldwide proliferation of emerging product standards.

Although Apple Computer may have lost control of its graphical user interface even as it became the market standard, it has proven to be a valuable source of top talent for other companies.

More than two dozen former Apple executives are running their own companies, from industry brand names like WebTV Networks, Intuit, and Macromedia, to a slew of start-ups. At least a dozen more Apple alumni are in senior posts in the engine rooms of giants like Sun Microsystems, Netscape Communications Corp., Microsoft Corp., and AT&T. "In the PC era, (Apple) definitely was the most influential company in terms of seeding talent."

Why so many Apple-bred CEOs? Being the first success among personal computer companies was a huge advantage, according to Floyd Kvamme, an Apple vice president from 1982 to 1984. "I think Apple is a good example that joining a revolution early is a good idea," said Kvamme, now a partner in Kleiner, Perkins, Caufield and Byers, a Menlo Park, New Jersey-based venture capital firm.[4]

Had Apple managed this process well, it might have had an entire stable of new ventures to buttress its position in the computer industry.

Setting strategy in a knowledge-enabled environment will become a game of seeking, evaluating, and selecting opportunities for which the rules of competition can be written to favor an emerging knowledge base or special competencies of a carefully tailored network of existing alliance partners. This is a game not of doing everything for oneself, but of learning how to partner, often in novel ways. Knowledge exchange—an activity formerly reserved to academics, industrial spies, and corporate rejects (renegades who might later become entrepreneurs)—will become an honored and vital profession in the emerging competitive environment.

step 3: securing

How is a company that expended time, energy, and resources shaping an industry or a market to ensure that it will not lose the value generated by its investment to a competitor? There is nothing automatic about realizing value. It does not simply fall into an innovator's hands. The last step of the strategy for speed, *securing,* involves extracting value for as long as possible without undermining the future. This is what Microsoft did: It held off the next generation to realize as much value as could be obtained from its DOS product, but not so long that its follow-on generation product, Windows, was late to market. Balancing value extraction and new innovation in a continuously changing world is as difficult as it is essential. Too many companies stop short of the final step of ensuring that all potential value is realized. To fully claim its prize, a firm must carefully avoid the many pitfalls in the global business environment; it must be prepared to boldly partner where no one has partnered before, to be able to visualize and direct the globalization journey.

points to remember

The e-Leader understands that:

- The old economy ran on the economic of exclusion, of barriers erected to keep competitors out.

- The new economy runs on the economics of inclusion, of knowledge-sharing and open exchange.

- Instead of erecting barriers, firms should encourage interaction; instead of trying to defend established positions, they should expect to reposition themselves through a dynamic process of continual innovation. With commercial advantage fleeting, only the quick survive.

- In this environment a firm's way of reviewing and changing direction must be very flexible and involve lots of people. This is best accomplished through the three-step process: seeking, shaping, and securing.

CHAPTER 10

opportunity-based strategy: the uniform strategic model

WHAT IF THE CONVENIENT AND FAMILIAR SEPARATION OF business processes into strategy formulation and execution should prove impossible to abandon? Can the new model be adopted by a firm that retains the bureaucratic process of strategy formulation? The answer to this question depends upon whether many executives in traditional firms can ever become effective e-Leaders. Fortunately, the answer is yes, at least to a degree—the new model can be applied, albeit imperfectly, in the old setting.

Having refocused from industries and competencies to opportunities and potentialities, the e-Leader proceeds to construct models that apply the new thinking. Only if they remain applicable in specific circumstances should old approaches be retained, appropriately supplemented and cast in a broader framework. The latter is achieved by means of a new, unified model of strategy formulation.

The unified strategic model (USM) integrates existing shareholder value and strategic change models with new front-end elements and contemporary management initiatives such as reengineering and value-chain analysis. It clarifies where what has been done conventionally fits into an overall strategic scheme and what has been left out or done only imperfectly. Value-chain, organizational change, and shareholder value are treated as modules in the larger model, each a fully articulated submodel of the USM.

Underlying the model and driving its application is the new way of thinking that emphasizes opportunity and potentiality. Strategy today is, or should be, concerned with identifying and selecting among opportunities, changing the organization so as to be able to seize these opportunities, and

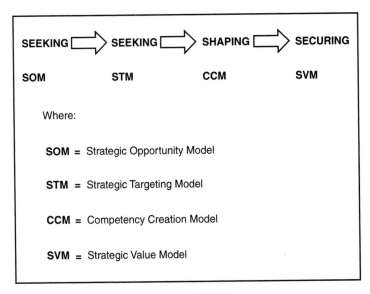

Figure 10-1 The Unified Strategic Model (USM)

optimizing the financial aspects of the new initiatives that result. Each of these four activities (see Figure 10-1) involves a separate and complex process that has a strategic orientation. In fact, various commentators and consultants have identified each as the core strategy to the exclusion of the others.

the strategic opportunity model

Largely missing from recent strategy discussions and poorly spelled out even when recognized, the strategic opportunity model (SOM) is the front end of the strategy model. Identifying opportunity has become crucial to strategy. Many winning companies are creating rather than simply serving markets. This is because growth generates shareholder value and market creation generates growth.

Today's other big winning strategy revolves around market restructuring—displacing existing providers with a dramatically different approach to the market. The best example are the great retail chains, franchises, and category-killers that displace existing firms. McDonald's by and large replaced diners; Wal-Mart, small-town department stores; Home Depot, downtown hardware stores; and CVS, corner drugstores. Opportunity consists of recognizing when an industry is ripe for restructuring.

Top executives instigate the search for opportunities by soliciting information and support within the organization and committing enthusiasm and resources. They thereby set in motion three simultaneous processes: a market review in conjunction with outsiders; idea gathering within the firm; and a technological application review. The first process is analytic; the second, fate (involving whomever has some notion); the third, selective and collective (brainstorming among individuals with particular expertise). These inputs feed a broader process of opportunity identification.

If an opportunity is in a business related to what a firm does, one track is followed; if it is in an unrelated business, a different track is taken. For opportunities in related businesses, it is generally presumed that a firm possesses key competencies. (If it does not, their absence must be addressed separately and directly.) An assessment of the organization's ability to seize the new opportunity will attempt to answer questions such as: "Can it do so successfully?" "If not, what is needed?" These questions should instigate a process of competence enhancement in which the applicability of new information technology, because it is the basis for creating or enabling strategic opportunities in many businesses today, is likely to play a large part. The amount of investment needed to capture the opportunity must then be determined, at which point the firm is positioned to pursue it through a process of managed change.

For opportunities in unrelated businesses, the process is only somewhat different. A careful analysis must be made of the new customers' needs and behaviors, and elements of the new business that will have to be supplied identified. The output of these stages suggests the new competencies the firm must develop if it is to be able to exploit the opportunity. These competencies must be secured one way or another, whether through purchase or acquisition, internal development, or partnering. If through the latter, potential partners must be identified. Finally, the level of investment must be determined and a process of managed strategic change inaugurated.

It is useful to think in terms of an opportunity spectrum at the identification stage. Strategy involves identifying high-potential points on the opportunity spectrum.

There are two types of customers in the world: individuals and organizations. In general, customer demand is driven by personal lifestyle mix (PLM), which creates opportunities by virtue of changing over time. PLM has been quite different in different countries, but is believed to be converging on that of the developed countries. Strategists examining PLM ask:

- **Where can a new product or service be introduced?**

- **Can an existing industry (that is, a component of consumer spending) be revolutionized?**

In general, organizational demand is driven by corporate input mix (CIM). "Corporate" is here understood to refer to government and not-for-profit entities as well. Opportunities are created in this realm as the proportion of spending shifts over time among elements of the mix. Because corporate is a derived, not final, demand, CIM should be considered in a context that involves its customers and its suppliers.

The first element of this context is the personal expenditure distribution, which is derived from the PLM; the second, the value-chain in which the corporation participates; and the third is the CIM itself. That is, each element of the

PLM defines an industry that has a value-chain that comprises corporations with associated spending mixes for the inputs they need to operate. For example, each of the companies that comprise the value-chain for the housing industry that exists to satisfy customers' need has an input spending pattern. Opportunities are created for sales to corporations both by changes in the personal expenditure mix (that is, the change in corporate demand derived from changes in consumer demand) and by shifts among firms along the value-chain.

The essence of strategy for a firm seeking to sell to individuals is to anticipate shifts in their lifestyle mix and, therefore, spending patterns. The essence of strategy for a firm seeking to sell to organizations is to anticipate changes in their customers' spending patterns or in the positioning of firms on the value-chain, and reposition so as to be able to seize opportunities created thereby.

Strategy can be *reactive* or *proactive*. Reactive strategies seek to capitalize on expected shifts in the PLM or CIM. Proactive strategies seek to create markets via new products or services that then become part of the PLM or CIM.

The most successful businesses are proactive strategists. They introduce new products or services and capitalize on the new markets they define (for example, the railway, the electric light, the telephone, the television, the personal computer). A new product or service, however, is not a sure thing. Some firms invent a product only to have others capitalize on it (for example, Microsoft Apple's innovation); others invent products and services for which there is no demand.

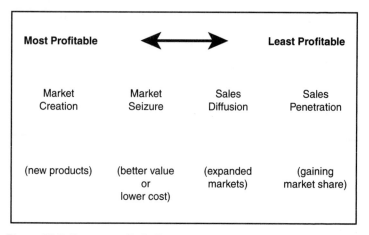

Figure 10-2 Opportunity Profit Spectrum

An adjunct to the opportunity spectrum, the opportunity profit spectrum (see Figure 10-2) identifies relative profitability of business opportunities.

the strategic targeting model

The strategic targeting model (STM) is a three-way matrix that relates goals to methods to contribution. Opportunities derived from the STM are analyzed for fit with a firm's goals and ability to execute (methods) and for their potential contribution to the firm's financial performance. Goals are often multiple and imposed on an executive or a firm (although firms sometimes set goals as well); methods involve both options and alternatives. Alternatives are necessary in order that the selection decision can be decoupled for the positioning decision (driven by the value-chain). Because the associated analytic process threatens to become expensive and lengthy, executives tend to be inclined to minimize the search for alternatives. Indeed, most strategy represents a leap to a particular course of action sans examination of alternatives, a shortcut often characterized as intuition. There is always an advantage to trying to generate alternatives and it can be done efficiently; it is not necessary to fully analyze all alternatives, only those that show promise. Potential contributions are measured by means of financial analyses of the various alternatives. Contributions must be risk-weighed (for example, globalization opportunities often incur added risk). The contribution should be maximized subject to constraints on a firm's ability to undertake new strategic initiatives.

the competency creation model

Efforts of behavioral scientists and organizational consultants to define the process whereby a company's organization and culture can be redirected to facilitate the pursuit of specific strategic business goals yielded the competency creation model (CCM). The model posits that a company's culture is not static, changing only in response to change initiatives, but evolves continuously and, hence, should be managed with strategic intent. This adds a second dimension to the STM, which usually focuses only on initiated change.

The direction of organizational change (in people, structure, culture, morale, and so forth) is driven by the results of the strategic targeting activity. This direction must be imposed on, introduced as a new element in, the evolution of the organization. Trying to direct evolutionary change might be perceived to be defensive; trying to direct the organization towards some new desired state, an offensive act.

If evolutionary change is in the desired direction, it can be reinforced in a variety of ways; if not, it must be challenged. Redirecting evolution involves establishing incentives that promote behavior consistent with the desired change, allaying employees' fears about risks that appear to be associated with the change, promoting voluntary acceptance of, and establishing disincentives for failure to accept, the proposed changes, incentives, and evaluating the consistency of the measures that are adopted. Inconsistencies must be rectified and the resulting incentives, penalties, and attitudinal interventions imposed to direct both evolutionary and desired changes.

The purpose of this module is to turn a business in the desired direction or, if it is on the desired path, ensure that it remains so.

the strategic value model

Having identified and targeted specific opportunities, developed competencies, and entered selected, potentially high-profit businesses, it is time to turn attention to deriving full value from the effort that has been made. The strategic value model (SVM), although originated as a business valuation model,[1] can be used to direct strategic thinking to the maximization of shareholder wealth as well as to value a company. The model's seen elements are described briefly. (See Table 10-1.)

1. When appropriate, value-chain analysis must be used to position a business unit correctly in its industry. This is possible for businesses in existing industries; it is extremely difficult or impossible for businesses that are Internet-based or in other ways novel.

2. Bottom-line contribution from the business must be maximized by rationalizing or reengineering its components to minimize cost.[2]

3. Value creation is maximized by creating virtual barriers to entry such as staying ahead by running ahead, engaging in alliances to forestall competitors, and gaining first-mover advantage.

4. Opportunities for expanding the existing business are defined, analyzed, and selected on a contribution analysis basis, whereby net present value is the standard of selection among competing investment opportunities. The traditional cash-cow/star matrix is applicable here. Some businesses merit further investment; some do not.

Table 10-1 The Strategic Value Model (SVM)

Stage 1	Repositioning, if appropriate	*Value-Chain Analysis*
Stage 2	Rationalization: creating efficiency	*Business Process Reengineering*
Stage 3	Creating barriers to competition, virtual and actual	*Competitive Analysis*
Stage 4	Optimization and expansion	*Present Value Analysis*
Stage 5	Financial restructuring	*Leverage and Cash Analysis*
Stage 6	Augmentation; mergers and acquisitions	*Contribution Analysis*
Stage 7	Portfolio analysis: what to keep; what to sell; what to buy	*Shareholder Value Analysis*

5. Opportunities for financial restructuring, increasing leverage, and improving cash management are explored and financial engineering exploited to add to the return from the business.

6. Consideration is given to augmenting the business via acquisitions, mergers, partnerships, or divestitures.

7. All elements of existing businesses are assessed as if they were part of a financial portfolio and a determination whether to hold or sell each made on the basis of its financial contribution and strategic relevance.

points to remember

The e-Leader recognizes that:

• Existing strategic models require a broader framework and new front end because (1) core competency analysis is too backward-looking (what about new competencies?) and (2) value-chain analysis is too myopic.

• The needed new framework is realized by casting existing models in a broader strategic process of opportunity identification (selection stage), value-chain/competency assessment (analysis stage), change direction or redirection (implementation stage), and value maximization with an underlying theme of strategy as execution.

• This new framework, termed the unified strategic model (USM), incorporates systematic approaches to opportunity identification, opportunity targeting, competency creation, and full-value realization.

• Companies can use the USM to capture the full potential of globalization.

leading for opportunity

to take advantage of the unparalleled opportunities afforded by globalization and electronic technology to build new business, the e-Leader must shift the focus of planning from the present to the future, from national markets to market creation in a global context, and from traditional approaches to new strategies for a connected world.

CHAPTER 11

potential is what matters most

AN E-LEADER WHO ORIENTS HIS OR HER COMPANY'S strategy towards opportunities and corporate potentialities will be well positioned to exploit the new economics. Revenues will be enhanced less by cutting costs than by enlarging the strategic framework to include a unified model that prefaces existing approaches—including value-chain and competency analysis—with models of opportunity identification and selection.

why the new economics demands a different approach to business

Yesterday—when time, distance, geographic features, and political boundaries constituted structural barriers around markets—the only option was to choose good markets, a task for which business executives relied on clever analysts. In recent years this market-seeking activity has benefited from the development of sophisticated country risk-analysis and global economic analysis techniques. Using the best tools of business strategy to assess market attractiveness, consultants evaluate business situations and advise clients to pursue the stars.

What limits most popular contemporary approaches—in particular, the competency models—is that they are backward-looking; they seek the key to a firm's future in its past. This brings to mind the story of the police officer who encounters a person searching for something under a lamppost.

> "What did you lose?" asked the officer.
> "My watch," the person replied.
> "Where did you lose it?" the officer asked.
> "Over there in the bushes."
> "Then why are you searching here?"
> "Because the light's better."

Why are today's strategists searching in the past for core competencies on which to build companies' futures? Because the light is better there. In today's fast-changing world, a company's future is not to be found in its past.

Today, traditional strategies are breaking down, necessitating the development of a new framework that better reflects the present context. This *forward-looking,* future-directed framework emphasizes opportunity seeking, market shaping, and barrier building to lock in as much value as possible, and resource optimization.

new business creation

New business creation flourished in the nineteenth century. Petroleum and telephone companies, railroads, and electric utilities generated enormous value for shareholders. With little but steady improvement in existing technologies, these companies became accustomed to fighting for position in well-established markets. A strategic mindset developed around positioning in existing industries and exploiting peculiar capabilities.

The close of the twentieth century saw a sudden burst of new market creation. Fast-food retailers (such as, McDonald's) were followed by discounters (for example, Wal-Mart) that were followed by category-killers (such as, Home Depot) in rapid succession. The rapid development of computer technology spawned a high-tech industry initially populated by giants such as IBM and DEC, later invaded by new entrants such as Intel and Microsoft, among a host of other firms. The end of the Cold War opened virtually the entire world to commerce, where upon new market creation could be driven by geography as well as technology.

Globalization and electronic networking have a surprisingly similar affect on strategy. Both afford opportunities to create new markets and to give rise to new competitors that alter the strategic situation. But associated with globalization is a great paradox that has no counterpart in electronic technology and that threatens to confuse strategy-making. The paradox is that although globalization is about geography, firms that embrace the world lose concern for the particulars of where they are located save for narrow business objectives. Strategically, geography becomes irrelevant, but management must still take account of distance and cultures.

redirecting attention

The need to reorient strategy in order to maximize shareholder value in the face of the explosion of opportunity for new business development seems more tractable when it is realized that it has been done before. That it is not a static concept is attested to by the contending schools of business strategy in evidence even today. Some strategic formulas emphasize stability and introspection; others, dynamism and accommodation to change. When contextual settings are shifting, these different approaches must fit together like pieces of a jigsaw puzzle. This chapter attempts to assemble the strategy jigsaw puzzle by adding to the existing pieces some important ones that have been missing.

The strategy based on barriers to entry is rendered increasingly irrelevant in the emerging electronically connected world. What is needed is a future-directed strategy premised on identifying and seizing short-lived opportunities. Executives should not construe the escalating speed and complexity of change to be, as some commentators are suggesting, a harbinger of impending chaos that will render planning a mechanism for reflexively coping with unpredictability. To propose the abandonment of planning would be a counsel of despair to top executives. Looking ahead is needed now more than ever as the time frame for implementing key elements of strategy—notably mergers and acquisitions, large-scale investment, and recruitment of top managerial talent—progressively collapses.

Speed of change does not necessarily correlate with degree of predictability. Paradoxically, a more rapid rate of change might yield a more predictable world.

Whatever the speed of change and degree of unpredictability, the more complex the environment, the more necessary the application of systematic thinking. But to reap the rewards of strategic thinking, corporate strategists must subscribe to a reformulation that ties planning more closely to action. Although at hand and potentially accessible to most executives, many observers have not yet seen it. Pundits who suggest that "strategic planning isn't strategic" are confusing a new paradigm with no paradigm. The demise of the mechanistic interpretation of planning heralds not a plunge into chaos, but the emergence of a novel, faster paced interpretation, a proactive rather than just reactive planning paradigm that enables executives to shape the future rather than wait for phenomena to emerge.

an opportunity-based strategic orientation

Although new business development is the most promising of the opportunities being served up by the globalized, electronically interconnected business environment, there are others. Globalization affords opportunities to shift position in a value-chain and cut costs via lower-cost production sites or greater production scale. Electronic commerce offers opportunities to alter supply chains in such significant ways that some analysts propose valuing e-commerce companies in terms of how much of an existing value-chain they destroy.

These opportunities will not be exploited—indeed, they will not even be discerned—by companies that pursue industry-based strategies that emphasize the structure and competitive factors of their particular industries or competency-based strategies that emphasize their core capabilities and assets. The companies that will create value from these opportunities will be those that embrace strategies that evolve from patterns that emerge from the aggregation of individual actions at all levels of the organization. These strategies will support quick responses to external forces, in particular, discontinuous changes in markets, products, or technologies.

The old strategic model was concerned with identifying markets and capturing as much of them as possible for other players. The new model revolves around delineating new markets, enlarging them by elaborating their electronic marketscapes, creating virtual barriers to entry, and maximizing the value that is realized. Firms in which the old strategic orientation persists look first at market attractiveness, then at their competencies. The new orientation is reflected in firms' zealous pursuit of opportunities for new businesses primarily through globalization and electronic networking initiatives.

With industry barriers of increasingly little consequence, as evidenced by Microsoft's incursion into financial services, managers must think in terms not of industries, but of market units. Managers who ask "Who are our competitors?" should discern three levels of competition: firms selling the same product; firms selling close substitutes; and firms competing for customers' attention with very different products. In general, the stronger a firm's position with respect to its closest competitors, the more it is concerned about more distant competitors. Coke, for example, is so strongly positioned in the soft-drink market that it evidences greater concern about producers of other beverages. Similarly, General Motors was once so strongly positioned in the American automotive market that it was concerned about the allocation of the consumer dollar among housing, food, and transportation.

When strategy emphasized being either low-cost or differentiated, exploiting core competencies (which implies that firms should not pursue value outside of what they have been doing), and developing focus and loyalty among customers in markets deemed to be attractive, the game was one of structural advantages, of securing market positions and protecting them from competitors. The new orientation of strategy is not to industry, competency, or evolutionary process, but to building and generating rapid growth in new markets with the object of maximizing gains in shareholder value. It focuses on networks of business relationships, not value-chains; on sets of opportunities, not existing competencies; and on developing a process by which to get creative initiatives right. It avoids problems that bedevil the old orientation in an environment of rapid change.

First, the opportunity-focused orientation is not industry-myopic like value-chain analysis. It is not constrained by existing industrial definitions.

Second, the new orientation is not conservative like the core competencies model. No matter what qualifications are offered, a fixation on competencies leads inevitably to the injunction "Stick to your knitting." In an age of globalization and electronic commerce, companies that take as their credo "We like to do this; we do it well; let's find a place we can do it" are virtually certain to be outflanked. Electronic commerce, for example, because it is not a core competency of any major corporation today, is likely to be ignored by top executives in formulating strategy. Moreover, when electronic commerce does intrude into a firm's strategy, it is almost invariably as an alternative to an existing core competency and, hence, likely to be rejected, not embraced. Top executives who embrace electronic commerce must abandon the current strategic orientation of their firms.

Third, the opportunity-focused orientation is forward-looking, not reactive as is the emergent-strategy approach. The question of the hour is not "What business are we in?" but "What business do we want to be in?" This involves focusing not on existing capabilities and what might be done with them, but on opportunities and how they might be seized. A firm should determine not what it is, but what it can be.

The best advice to top executives is: Forget your industry! Send your production and government relations people to industry meetings. When you go to meetings, look for where you can make money and join that game.

the new approach follows the new economics

The new strategic orientation reflects the new economics. The new game is one in which market position cannot be protected behind national or economic barriers, in which structural advantages gain less than executional advantage.

In the absence of traditional barriers to entry offered by distance, national boundaries, capital investment, patents, and so forth, virtual barriers must be created to maximize market potential. Utilizing the Internet, on which every new customer is free, can drive costs towards zero and push potential value upwards without bound.

thinking about opportunity

How a person thinks might seem a topic too abstract for practical executives, but mental predilections are absolutely crucial to practical outcomes. Rigidity in thinking can determine the outcome of a strategic study long before the details have been worked through. One is put in mind of a military force that, when presuming the attack cannot come from one direction, strengthens its defenses on the others. Businesses, too, can be outflanked.

Strategists who accept without question two of today's tenets of strategy—exploit core competencies and maintain focus—may well deprive their companies of lucrative opportunities not as a consequence of careful analysis, but because key alternatives are simply ruled out by rigid thinking.

Strategy in a rapidly changing business landscape needs to be concerned with business opportunities and organizational potentialities. In a future-directed firm what is done now is less important than what can be done. Companies must be conceived in terms not only of what they are, but of what they might become. Wall Street does this in a certain narrow range. Its analysts are able to extrapolate the growth rate for an innovative company and price its shares to a degree on what is expected to come. But it is rare for the Street to increase the value of a company because it might move into a different business. That is precisely what company strategists ought to be doing—searching for new arenas in which the company can grow more rapidly or improve margins. To some degree this has always been a function of strategy, but in a more slowly changing world searching out new forums for business was overshadowed by other aspects of strategy, including positioning in an existing value-chain and exploiting core competencies.

The market space at the business frontier is one of simultaneously shifting opportunities that are given shape only when firms seize on some aspect of them and thereby redefine the opportunity space for all. The future-directed firm is a bundle of potentialities that, exploited selectively by its executives, define the immediate future and determine financial success or failure.

potentiality as planning

Planning is about turning potentialities into realities by choosing the game to play and determining where and how to play it. It is not about identifying the opportunities that best fit the potentialities, which is the error of competency-based strategy. The ideal approach is to find the best opportunity a company has the potential to exploit. A company's potentialities are certainly related to its core competencies, but in a derivative way. Core competencies are what a firm is; potential is what it can become. Planning based on core competencies is too likely to ignore potentialities.

The proper role of planning is to establish the timing and correct sequence of activities, including the assembly of resources, to seize an opportunity. In this sense, the strategies of even the biggest companies must become more entrepreneurial.

new skills for planners

In addition to knowledge about the core competencies of their firm, and the shape of the value-chain in particular industries, planning staff need to possess three new skills:

- adeptness at recognizing opportunities;
- perceptiveness with respect to the changing map of world business; and
- the capacity to follow and understand developments in information and communication technology and their possible strategic applications.

These three skills are related. An opportunity-focused strategist finds potentialities, the key (but not exclusive) drivers of which are globalization and electronic technology. Hence, all three skills impel strategists towards a broader sweep of the horizon in search of their companies' futures.

Planning is thus about glimpsing opportunities beyond the horizon and avoiding being blindsided. Remarked John Wellesley, Duke of Wellington: "All strategy consists in trying to see what's on the other side of the hill."

the emergence of mega-competition

Observers of the electronically connected world have focused on the virtual corporation without recognizing that it is attended by a new level of competition, that between industries, which we term *mega-competition*. The virtual corporation not only enables small firms in a value-chain to combine to challenge larger firms, but for value-chains in an industry to combine to challenge other industries for customers' attention.

What is seen today is only the beginning. Trade associations might eventually link producers, suppliers, and even unions to facilitate competition with other industries.

Customers' consumption capacity is finite and allocated among competing alternatives. A family will spend more on housing, less on food; more on entertainment, less on clothing; and so forth. Market analysts presume that providers' allocations will not vary much over time. It might be made to vary quite a bit, however, as a consequence of determined marketing by virtual corporations.

Interindustry competition exists in both consumer and industrial markets. Consider, for example, the competition among brick and wood and structural steel for building; between broadcast and cable companies for program delivery; among aluminum, soft pack, and steel (the tin can) for packaging. Or consider the apparel industry which is struggling to attract consumer attention from electronic gadgetry, new automobiles, and the rising tide of entertainment and travel. The virtual corporations that link elements of the apparel supply chain will soon be competing at the market level for the consumer's dollar.

The virtual corporation that links the final product firms in a supply chain so as to make the industry appear to be one large entity competes with equivalent virtual corporations in other industries for consumers' attention and expenditure.

points to remember

The e-Leader must:

- **Reorient strategy towards the future.**
- **Focus on opportunities.**
- **Not just segment a market, but create one.**
- **Shape the marketplace.**
- **Build barriers to lock in value.**
- **Maximize value realization.**

CHAPTER 12

crisis in
corporate leadership

UNEXPECTED DEPARTURES OF TOP EXECUTIVES HAVE BEEN much in the news in recent years. Whatever the cause—a decision by the board of directors or deep differences with a firm's board or current chief executive—mishires and quits seem at an all-time high, in numbers, size of the companies involved, and attendant visibility and publicity. This is because too many executives have failed to become e-Leaders.

Expectations of top executives today are enormous. Wall Street has never been more unforgiving of missteps in corporations' quarterly performance. Insistence that executives' sole objective must be to maximize shareholder wealth opens the executives of firms that fail to perform as expected to investor fury and shareholder-initiated lawsuits. Add to these expectations: pressure to adopt a global mindset; increasingly diverse and divergent firm cultures and employees complicating the process of management; questions of the effectiveness and loyalty of telecommuters occasioned by the emergence of the virtual organization; and the return (if any) on large financial investments in information technology.

How well prepared are executives to meet these challenges by becoming e-Leaders? What executives learn early in their careers managing departments and business units does not necessarily help them in their top leadership roles. That many executives are employing personal coaches, many of whom have little business experience, suggests lack of preparation for certain key aspects of the job. A liberal education—because it prepares a person to champion a corporate culture, deal with politicians and foreign governments, and represent a firm in multiple public forums—would be a splendid background. But few executives in the United States and Japan receive such an education owing to the many technical hurdles interposed on the way to the top. In Europe, in contrast, liberal education is the way to the top, but technical competence is slighted on the way. American, German, and Japanese firms have drawn strength from their executives' technical capability, to the disadvantage of firms led by liberally educated executives. Clearly, today's best prepared top executive is a technically competent individual with a strong liberal arts grounding. The implication is clear: It is incumbent on firms to provide compensatory liberal education, and liberal arts education or technical skills development depending on the prevailing emphasis of local institutions.

In fact, many of today's top executives who did run a business unit earlier in their careers probably could not run that same unit today. But to say that lack of preparation lies at the root of executive failure is not to say that more preparation will readily solve the problem. The dichotomous nature of career paths to the top restricts preparation. One path, via a sequence of positions in the same function, produces top-level executives without comprehensive knowledge of their companies; the other path, via a succession of general management positions running business units, produces top-level executives with an excess of operations experience, but ill-prepared with respect to strategy and overall leadership.

Firms that have difficulty making their own leadership can buy it. Top executives can be hired from outside, from a consulting company or another firm, perhaps in a different industry directly into the top job. Breadth of view is anticipated to compensate for lack of firm-specific knowledge, but this deficit is a formidable obstacle to an externally recruited executive.

The recency of the lattice as an arrangement for conducting business poses a special leadership problem for which no amount of experience has prepared executives, namely, the task of building a pipeline of people able to run it. Lattices are not merely communication systems. They comprise different administrative and operational characteristics, both formal and informal, that must be rendered somehow compatible and integrated—no small task and one relatively new.

forces that shape the
globally attuned executive

The globally attuned executive is shaped by the forces that are driving global business as well as by other forces specific to executive jobs. Among the most significant forces of globalization are the complexity of diverse nationalities and cultures and attendant demand for a new mindset; the emergence of virtual organizations with the attendant problem of managing unseen people; mergers and acquisitions with the accompanying challenge of integrating organizations and cultures; and changing generations with the shift from willing workers to challenging workers.

A further complicating factor is the tightening of U.S. labor markets for the first time in decades. The long economic upswing that has inflated share values is now transforming the longstanding labor surplus into labor shortages, a situation U.S. firms have not faced for 30 years. This environment poses sudden new challenges to executives responsible for attracting and retaining top talent.

Do tightening labor markets foretell a shift to a sort of free agency in the economy as a whole? Will rising compensation cut profits and bring about a failure to meet Wall Street's expectations for earnings per share? Can the challenge of labor shortages be met by a return to the practice of corporate loyalty through employment security?

In late 1980 IBM was roundly criticized for its no-layoff policies and abandoned them. For decades, however, its culture of corporate loyalty had enabled the company to hire and retain top talent at low cost. Wholesale downsizing in the 1990s changed the scene. Can today's corporate leaders raise the phoenix of loyalty from its ashes? It will not be easy. Today's workers temper aspirations with cynicism. As eager as the workers who have gone before them to belong to a tight-knit organization that attends to their welfare and career opportunities, they nevertheless suspect executive-level management by and large to be prepared to terminate their employment at a moment's notice for no more than the chance to push a single dollar to the bottom line.

A deeply emotional generation born of political disillusionment and economic insecurity, they enter an economic environment greatly improved over the past decade still bearing the scars of downsizing. Relative to their predecessors, these people, anxious to believe that their leaders care, feel more than they think; seeking reassurance in communication, talk more than they act. Workers suddenly more important to employers facing labor shortages are likely to be more assertive and less willing to accept direction.

"Just give me my PC and leave me alone" is an attitude widely observed among engineers in high-technology firms. As described in Chapter 9, Sun Microsystems almost killed its Java product in the cradle when it threatened to halt Internet surfing by its engineers. To stem the diversion of attention from duty—Sun executives saw it as designing workstations—managers rankled engineers with what seemed to the latter short-sighted, misdirected policy. The company verged on chaos, or so its executives thought. Years later Sun was still trying to gain control over the activities of its engineers.

But as is so often the case in business, what seems chaotic is simply not understood. What Sun executives perceived to be a crisis of discipline was in fact the loud knocking of opportunity. Fortunately for the company, its engineers heard it and, because they were in high demand and not easily replaceable, they were able to persuade the executives to listen. What Sun executives slowly came to realize was that the Internet might challenge the dominance of the personal computer. From that evolved the notion that a programming language might be developed to facilitate the transfer of applications between the Internet and devices simpler than personal computers. Sun developed the language, named it Java, and set out to try to change the world of computing.

No less than it needs controls, a company needs to be attuned to change. When control seems to be slipping, it may be that the world has become different and we no longer understand it. To executives reared in the command and control economies of the old Communist bloc, for example, a free market seems chaotic. Production and demand seem often mismatched, with shortages of what is in demand and much produced for which there is no demand. Balance seems always just out of reach, with markets inefficient and directionless.

Yet markets are characterized not by chaos, but by order arising out of their nature, as executives long experienced in them understand. Markets trade inefficiencies in the small for efficiencies in the large; the invisible hand of price coordinates apparently disparate decision-making; surpluses and shortages are resolved by the profit-motive. The market that seems so chaotic is, in fact, a highly coordinated mechanism.

This is true even of the apparently chaotic world share markets, which tend to be predictable when the rules of the exchanges, flows of information, and motivations of the participants are understood.

So it is in business. Globalization and the connected world will seem chaotic to those used to something different. They are likely to perceive the status quo as simple and comprehensible, the new world of business as complex and indecipherable. The truth will be that the new world, albeit different, is in its own way simple, understandable, and comprehensible. The limiting factor is not the new world, but those too firmly attached to the old.

alternative designs for creating the new leadership

Demands on executives are both economic and human. The global business environment requires skills of a different order and the changing attitudes of people a different leadership approach. Executives who view the transitions made by successful companies as discrete events will not keep their companies moving as the environment changes further still. Leadership is less a matter of surmounting discrete challenges than a process of continual change.

Some commentators despair of companies finding executives who can master the challenges just described. They long instead for an alternative form of leadership. Their concern centers on the job at the top, but is it safe for a firm to entrust its future to an individual?

Alternatives exist. U.S. firms, like many of their European and Japanese counterparts, might be managed by teams. For the American model of the CEO as boss, the foreign model substitutes the first in a team of near equals. Or, as in the military model, top commands might be rotated among executives. (The United States's Pacific Fleet rotates commanders at least every 30 months, thereby avoiding burnout and cultivating a corps of experienced commanders.)

However appropriate these forms might be for some firms, they are unlikely to gain widespread acceptance. Wall Street prefers the single-point accountability that is the hallmark of the American CEO and Wall Street's standards are increasingly those of capital markets generally. The boss is in charge and accountable to the board and investors for the firm's performance on his or her watch.

The paradox to which this gives rise is that companies in which advancement is increasingly in the context of shared responsibilities, prospective CEOs must suddenly break ranks with teamwork in order to enter, with little direct preparation for doing so, the rarified atmosphere of sole accountability. Never before has leadership at the top been such a different animal from that elsewhere in the organization.

the emotional executive

It is incumbent on each executive to personally develop a fit to his or her context. This top leadership is less science than art.

But no one develops entirely in this way. Rather, people are molded early in life by events and experiences that later determine their fitness for top leadership.

Given the vagaries and vicissitudes of personal development, whether a person fits or not is a matter as much of fate as preparation.

How individuals handle key events in their personal lives—whether, for example, they rise above or are crushed by emotional losses; accept or are paralyzed by risk—has a bearing on how they will fare, and perform, in a top leadership role. Ideally, what is wanted is an individual who possesses sufficient emotional strength to function as a firm's alter ego. This is, in fact, a useful way to construe top executives: as individuals with qualities of character—some admirable in contexts other than business, some not—which permit him or her to serve as the single expression of personality for the people who make up a firm.

Owing in part to the cynicism and skepticism that pervade the "downsized" generation, in many instances executives today seem to need to be as much emotional as executive officers since they are called on to inspire those workers. Leadership today is as much about emotion as about administration; more, as should have been made clear by the discussion of Sun Microsystems, about inspiring than about directing. "If you can't energize other people," remarked Jack Welch to his managers, "you're of no use to GE as a leader." To do so, an executive must cultivate a public personality in the manner of a celebrity. Indeed, with business's advance into the world spotlight, the press is increasingly treating executives as celebrities.

With the economy strong and share prices at or near all-time highs, executives perceive themselves to be doing a good job, and they are. But employees' as well as Wall Street's expectations are high. Jeff Sonnenfeld surveyed CEOs who characterized themselves as effective agents for change and saw themselves as defining a vision of the future and pushing people out the door to create it, and employees who described CEOs who did too little to enable the change process neglected to define roles for subordinates, provided little or no support to subordinates needing to build new skills, and failed to sustain the impetus for change over time.[1]

To energize employees, executives must stand for something more than shareholder value; they must demonstrate a new kind of integrity, a new way of working. They must establish a new kind of balance between themselves and those in the organization.

People follow leaders with whom they feel emotionally connected, who are decisive in a way that demonstrates that they are in touch with their employees as well as with the business context.

Facing inward, towards their employees, executives must be emotional officers; facing outward, towards their boards, investors, and others outside their firms' performance, they must be equity officers. Facing both directions simultaneously is the crux of top executives' special responsibilities. In one direction they are diplomats to government officials, lobbyists within countries, community leaders, and links to key customers and suppliers; in the others they are strategy setters, developers of executive talent (through assignments to promising managers), and key motivators of the rank and file.

In their dealings with what might be called its foreign relations, a firm's top executives are its link to the capital markets. Some executives might even be thought of as tribunes governing far-flung provinces on behalf of their respective empires. Executives are the representatives of the investors who are sovereign in, but distant from, the firm. They are not the expression of the firm to the capital markets, but of the capital markets to the firm. How often in recent years have executives echoed a statement made by a top officer of an American firm conducting yet another downsizing: "I hate what the markets are making us do to our employees." Yet that was their responsibility.

lead thyself

To cope with the tremendous stress born of investors' and employees' high expectations and the pressures of a rapidly changing world, executives must be adept at managing their own person, what psychologists term their personal process. Fortunately, the new generation of executives assuming leadership in many companies are baby boomers finally reaching the top spots who share with the rest of their generation a facility with personal concerns. These executives do not view personal matters as evidence of weakness and irrelevant to business leadership, as did so many of their predecessors.

Nor is the importance to business of intuition—a sort of pattern recognition and response formulation mechanism that is the largely unconscious consequence of experience—lost on this new generation of top executives. Flights of successful intuition can be usefully analyzed to discover the principles that they embody. It must be remembered, however, that intuition is a two-edged sword. Those inclined always to put intuition ahead of reflection are more likely to be misled by faulty assumptions, especially about how others will behave.

The importance of a cool head in top leadership cannot be overestimated. "The first quality of a General-in-Chief," remarked no less than Napoleon, "is to have a cool head which receives exact impressions of things, which never gets heated, which never allows itself to be dazzled, or intoxicated, by good or bad news."[2]

steps to developing the global business associate

People make the difference in successful globalization and what makes the difference in people is a global mindset.

The Global Mindset Is Implicit in a Multiple Nationality Context: Exploit It!

It is possible, albeit difficult, expensive, and unnecessary, to develop a global mindset in people of a single nationality. Still companies do it. Firms that continue, after decades of international experience, to move more rather than fewer home country persons into positions in foreign subsidiaries, are resisting the logic of globalization on people side.

It is, in fact, easier to cultivate a global mindset in people drawn from different nations who embody as a group much of the knowledge and experience relevant thereto. The degree to which companies are becoming, in their executive suites and managerial cadres, more international remains unclear.

counter the "actor" syndrome: compensate for overspecialization

Much of the value of a global mindset is lost if people in an organization do not work closely together. Professional actors tend to find it difficult to work closely with those outside their specialty, yet we are today building organizations of actors and trying to get them to work together closely and flexibly. When firms merge, for example, it is today's common practice for the consolidated firm to retain the best people in their respective specialties, and then be astonished at the difficulty of fostering cooperation among them.

Management meetings in such firms follow a predictable course. Presenters, in their turn, make a case for the considerable importance of this or that development in their respective fields, little heeded by others who sit dwelling on the importance of their own specialties. No real information exchange occurs at such meetings. Overspecialization confounds efforts to foster cooperation around a global mindset in today's organizations. However valuable communication might be to a firm, people who do not listen to others most of the time find it difficult to do so even some of the time.

one way or another, expose people to the world

Many people are poorly informed about what is happening outside their countries. Corporations often seek to remedy this among high-potential managers through classroom courses that review international economic and political developments. Albeit useful, such courses do little more than open a door to a global mindset. Following up, as some companies do, with subscriptions to periodicals that cover international development is useful to the extent that recipients read them, which few do. Assignments abroad are perhaps the most effective way to familiarize managers with global business. Only a year or two in a particular part of the world might yield a multinational mindset but is hardly likely to precipitate a global one.

What is needed, especially for those who are never assigned abroad, is a more comprehensive effort to engage people in a community within the firm that is concerned with global business. Individuals should initially be tutored or mentored, later be invited to participate in international projects, and still later tutor others. The objective, of course, is to evolve a cadre of decision-makers for whom consideration of opportunities and challenges the world over is routine.

The process by which a global mindset can be cultivated in the absence of foreign assignments includes the following steps:

1. **Help individuals begin to understand on a personal basis what it means to have a global mindset. Build bridges**

between them and others in the firm who are knowledgeable about international developments.

2. Include individuals in communities of managers or professionals who deal with global aspects of business issues.

3. Provide opportunities for individuals to participate in projects or issue analyses related to a global business activity.

4. Provide opportunities for individuals to head projects related to, or make presentations about, global aspects of business issues.

5. Provide opportunities for individuals to explain to others in the firm the meaning and significance of a global mindset.

It educates individuals and provides opportunities for them to discuss global issues of significance to the firm with communities of other people and, ultimately, to apply their accumulating knowledge.

It thus counters the greatest threat to developing a global mindset, inattention, which can be a consequence of nothing in an individual's job setting reinforcing the importance of a global perspective.

points to remember

1. The e-Leader knows that both the business and human environments of firms are becoming more challenging. As a result e-Leaders:

   must be capable of leading people of different cultures, races, and genders in the context of increasingly complex political and technological environments; and

must be emotional as well as equity officers of firms.

2. Leading will increasingly require decisiveness coupled with delegation, a balance that is achieved only by exceptional people.

3. The most difficult leadership problem for many e-Leaders will be managing themselves.

making arrays, mindset, and speed work for you

The accelerating rate of change in the global market space imposes a blunt new reality: Firms can no longer expect to own everything they need to conduct their businesses. Instead, the e-Leader must demonstrate that his or her company is the premier provider of a particular critical competence in a value-chain and partner with other companies that demonstrate themselves to be premier providers of complementary competencies. Profitability will depend on ceaselessly identifying new pockets of value and lining up and sustaining relationships with partners worldwide.

CHAPTER 13

avoiding pitfalls

THE E-LEADER STRESSES THE IMPORTANCE OF PURSUING A regimen of seeking, shaping, and securing to set his or her company on the path to superior performance in the global economy of the twenty-first century. The path, however, is not without risks. Let's identify—in the context of companies that have avoided or overcome them—eight common pitfalls of which e-Leaders must be wary.

pitfalls in seeking

retaining a national mindset

Companies often remain national because their executives, unable to make the mental leap to global mindset, remain wedded to that construct. Their manufacturing and distribution systems remain national in scope even as their web sites draw international orders. Other companies operate as multinationals, but limit their scope of opportunity in the larger arena by continuing to perceive themselves as national entities.

Companies that teeter on the edge of, rather than confidently plunge headlong into, globalization often fail to grasp the opportunities open to them in the larger context. This is why mindset matters.

Consider multinational companies clearly associated with particular nation-states; for example, Boeing with the United States, British Telecom with the United Kingdom, and Siemens with Germany. Their shareholders, or the shareholders of the institutions that own their shares, the people they employ, both directly and indirectly (through close supplier relationships), and their customers being from many nations, these companies are in a sense already nonnational. Yet people refer to Boeing as American, Siemens as German, and British Telecom as British. What makes people think of these companies as national?

What makes an American company that has extensive non-American operations still an American company is in part firm history ("This is where the company started"); in part, a legality ("This is where the firm is incorporated"); in part, location ("This is where our headquarters is situated"); and in part, the composition of the executive team ("We're all Americans"). None of these considerations is immutable. History cannot be changed, but it need not dictate the present. Legal incorporation does not constrain mindset and can be changed if desired. Headquarters is becoming less central to a firm, as administrative activities are dispersed and distributed and top executives spend more of their time traveling between customers and suppliers as well as company sites, a development that calls to mind a remark made by General George Burnside upon taking command of the Army of the Potomac in 1862: "My headquarters will be in the saddle." (A wag is said to have quipped: "It appears to me that the general's headquarters will be where his hindquarters ought to be.") Only the composition of the executive team seems to constrain transcendence of a national mindset, yet even persons of the same nationality, provided they concern themselves with international developments, are often able to manage effectively outside their native countries. What makes a company American, then, is that its executives think of it as American, nothing more. It is a self-imposed limitation.

The thought process whereby a company's executives begin to think of it less as a national and more as a global entity is akin to that whereby the English settlers in North America began to think of themselves less as English persons in America than as Americans and Canadians. The latter process extended over more than one hundred years. It has taken time, too, for executives to begin to make their transitions.

There is a business reason for making this mental transition, perhaps best exemplified by the declaration by Boeing's top executive that that firm has ceased to be an American and become a global firm. In some of the corners of the globe Boeing's identification with America is a hindrance. Boeing's recognition that it has transcended the national boundaries that constrained it for years is relatively recent. Like the transition from Englishman to American, the mental transition from American to global company has taken a long time.

In nations with histories devoid of a transference of self-conception such as Americans and Canadians experienced, it is more difficult to imagine companies transcending their national origins to become global. Executives of some European and Asian companies—among them Shell and Holvis—are nevertheless engaged in this transition.

misunderstanding opportunities

We are to a greater extent than most realize creatures of our environment. We develop a sense of what is expected of us and of what constitutes reality and truth in our particular physical context. We expect things to happen in certain ways and become suspicious when they do not. What we sometimes fail to realize is that outside this setting, we tend to be much less adept. Thus it is that businesspeople operating outside of their native context sometimes make errors that they would be very unlikely to make at home.

Efforts to mislead, for example, North American mining company executives about gold deposits that would never succeed were they operating on their home turf, might go undetected in a foreign context such as Indonesia which, being quite different, causes key signals to be missed. Similarly, an American company that fails to understand OPEC's workings might misvalue energy assets, a mistake it would never have made at home where the

Texas Railroad Commission establishes prices for domesti-
cally produced oil. Or, as happened to Sony, a Japanese
electronics company that misunderstands the culture and
accounting of Hollywood might purchase properties that
turn out to have little value, led by executives of little
integrity.

being the same company in a different place

Being global does not mean, as some businesspeople seem
to think, doing the same thing everywhere in the same way.
Instead, it might mean adjusting aspects of a business to the
particular conditions of a country. It is possible, and often
advantageous, to be global and be perceived to be local.

Its policy of not only selling, but also locating manufacturing and research and development facilities in Europe
and employing European managers and executives led
Europeans (including many government officials) to come to
view IBM as a European, not American, company. It being
central to quality and cost control, McDonald's, when it
went to Europe, tried to keep as much of its standard operating practice as possible but it accepted European mores by
including wine and beer in its beverage offerings.

At the core of successful globalization is a balancing act:
Which aspects of product, service, management, and operations should be localized? Which should be uniform
globally? Value-based management raises the question: Is it
possible to run a global company with a uniform set of values? Certainly some major companies have done so. IBM
for many years operated globally on three basic principles:

pursuit of excellence, best service to the customer, and respect for the individual.

What is common about these examples is that promulgated values are few in number, broad in scope, and positive in direction. Successful global companies do not—except in unusual circumstances—enforce corporate values over social, religious, or national convictions.

making inappropriate choices

Firms often enter foreign markets in cooperation with partners engaged via joint ventures, agents, or acquisitions. Many candidates are likely to offer themselves or be recommended. But which is the right partner?

Neither SmithKline nor Beecham, two mid-size pharmaceutical companies, had favorable prospects in the 1980s. U.K.-based Beecham needed a greater marketing presence outside Britain. Development failures had left SmithKline's U.S.-based, physician-oriented sales force without new products to sell.

"As we looked at our competitors," recalled Bob Bauman of SmithKline, "and the huge costs of research and development . . . I felt that to move up into a world-class position in the field meant looking for the opportunity for a merger."[1] Beecham's Henry Wendt was also looking for a partner. In 1989 the firms merged. There was little overlap in product lines or geographic coverage, the merger being intended not to cut costs, but to create opportunities. It was yet another version of the globalization journey: a merger of equals to gain scale and presence in the global marketplace.

pitfalls in shaping

failing to sequence properly

Firms begin in one country and journey to others on their way to globalization. Some are successful; some are not. Some are successful quickly; some only at length and at great cost. A major source of difficulty is failure to appreciate the proper sequence of steps in the globalization journey.

British Petroleum's decades-long effort to establish a global brand name in the retail market for gasoline and other oil products reflected a failure to sequence properly. A new chief executive officer decided in the early 1990s that BP's problem lay in its management style and structure. When he tried to reorganize the company from a complex line-of-business arrangement with 70 or more national headquarters into a less hierarchical, less country-specific networked company, financial performance weakened. His successor (appointed upon his dismissal two years later) launched a number of initiatives seeking to recover lost ground. The outsourcing and partnering that followed eventually led to a radical proposition—that it should partner with Mobil to sell oil products and gasoline in Europe, thereby freeing itself to concentrate on doing what it does best—finding oil around the globe. With this change in focus, the networked organization suddenly began to function more effectively and sales and profits recovered. What BP had done was stumble over sequencing; business rationalization needed to precede, not follow, organizational reform.

Robert Horton had sought to transform BP into a more flexible global company and expected strategy and performance improvements to follow, but he had key elements out of sequence. Sir David Simon and John Browne, on the other hand, got the sequencing right by placing strategy before structure, clearly defining roles for different layers in the organization, and delegating within that framework.

failing to partner across sectors

Americans are by and large accustomed to a business world in which government and nonprofit entities play little role. This is far less the case abroad.

pitfalls in securing

failing to leverage assets

The greatest advantage of globalization is the opportunity to leverage (or arbitrage) a firm's assets, both tangible and intangible. This can only occur, however, if a firm is properly organized and led. The structure appropriate to a domestic market may not be appropriate to a global one and leadership styles that are successful at home may not be abroad.

failing to justify globalization to wall street

One of the most value-enhancing acts a firm can do is establish a global presence. We emphasized earlier the premium Wall Street applies to the shares of global firms. But a globalization initiative can backfire if Wall Street considers the effort ill-conceived and likely to drain rather than enhance a firm's performance. Too often firms fail to convince Wall Street that their efforts abroad are strategically-based, well-conceived, and well-implemented.

Ingersoll Rand was an interesting contrast in the early 1990s. The heavy-equipment manufacturer had been an exporter in the 1960s and 1970s, until the oil shocks and rising dollars undercut its foreign market. Going global was crucial to being able to insulate itself from such market disruptions. Through carefully chosen locations abroad and a well-considered diversification, the company reduced its dependence on cyclical industries, stabilized its earnings growth, and, by making sure that Wall Street understood these initiatives, raised its multiple and share price well above those of its competitors.

points to remember

For e-Leaders seeking global advantages major pitfalls can loom in each of the following three steps:

seeking

- Retaining a national mindset
- Misunderstanding opportunities
- Being the same company in a different place
- Making inappropriate choices

shaping

- Failing to sequence properly
- Failing to partner across sectors

securing

- Failing to leverage assets
- Failing to justify globalization to Wall Street

CHAPTER 14

embarking on the three-step journey

Previous chapters considered shifts in the responsibilities of e-Leaders in companies seeking to create value through global business activities:

- Develop business opportunities via the business array.

- Adapt the company to a new form of organization: the global business lattice.

- Cultivate in the management and employees via changes in the company's culture a global mindset.

- Adopt a new approach to business planning via three integrated steps executed at the operating unit level.

responsibilities of e-leaders

reconfigure the firm beyond the matrix

Many international companies structure operations according to a *product-geography* matrix. Global companies transform such matrices into true networks by pushing more authority outward from corporate center (decentralize) and downward from the executive suite (delegate) and by empowering local managers to be more responsive to customers and others across multiple markets. Practical implementation tactics include:

1. freeing local managers to establish alliances that will position the company to exploit perceived opportunities to generate value,

2. establishing profit centers as the company's "unit of action,"

3. abolishing nonessential corporate mandates, and

4. measuring local managers on the basis of results, not actions.

develop approaches for leveraging intangible assets such as knowledge across cultural boundaries

To ensure that employees drawn from a widening range of cultures and locations interact effectively by facilitation communication, globalizing companies must address the ambiguity that tends to accompany greater diversity through investments in the development and maintenance of a common language and suitable infrastructure. Practical implementation tactics include: cultural development and reinforcement programs; multiple, cross-unit personnel assignments; and incentives, enabled by groupware-based systems, to capture and share "lessons learned."

instill among leaders at all levels a global mindset

A tendency towards "localizaton" in the networks of globalizing companies should be addressed by making greater use of reporting and control systems to instill a "global" mindset.

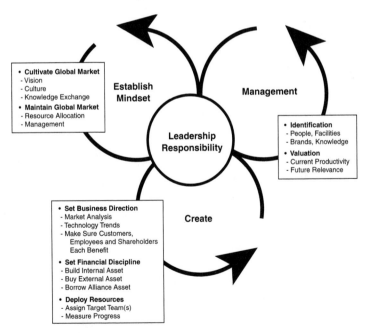

Figure 14-1 The Role of e-Leadership

These systems should be populated with financial (profit, cost) or operational (scrap rate, customer satisfaction index) metrics that yield similar decision-making signals regardless of the source of information. Recognize that localization occurs at the headquarters level as well and try to ensure that top-level decisions also reflect global priorities. Practical implementation tactics include reliance on "standardized" reporting systems capable of generating site-specific performance data that can be aggregated or compared across sites. The role of e-Leadership is putting it all together as diagrammed in Figure 14-1.

why firms seldom, and how they might, realize full value

Implicit in the three-step process of seeking, shaping, and securing is that executives think and formulate strategy differently. The process calls for reorganizing the firm by building strategic competence into business units and assembling resources via alliances and partnerships. To flourish in business arrays means firms must move faster, decentralize further, and build extranets that embody strategic objectives. Such firms will exhibit the following characteristics:

- *Asynchronous, yet interdependent, operation.* Because a typical enterprise operates across all 24 time zones, key executives never have immediate (synchronous) access to all assets, people, and facilities. Multinationals solve the attendant problem of control through duplication. Can a more efficient way of exercising authority be found?

- *Cultural integration (global mindset)*. Attempts by internationalizing companies to embrace multiple local cultures can tear them apart. Multinationals often impose their "culture of origin"—accepting distance from the local milieu as a cost of doing business. Can a global enterprise absorb local cultures and preserve sufficient commonality to sustain a global mindset?

- *Alliances readiness*. The discipline of economic value suggests that scarce capital should be allocated only to activities performed more efficiently in-house than by other companies. Activities should not be purchased for the sole purpose of "controlling" them, hence, the need for alliances. How can a global enterprise ensure that its structure will be flexible enough to accommodate rapid reconfiguration when existing alliance partners no longer deliver value?

- *Effective management of rapidly depreciating knowledge capital*. Globalism and globalization will render the global market space chaotic. With opportunities likely to vanish as quickly as they emerge, speed of execution will be essential to success. How can a global enterprise ensure that it will be able to move and use value-creating information immediately?

- *Assured customer responsiveness*. Would-be global enterprises must be capable of turning customers into partners; the future will be a game of setting standards for others. Traditional functional hierarchy fragments customer focus; it assigns customers specifically to marketing and permits other functions to effectively ignore them. How can a global enterprise impose market discipline and sustain customer focus throughout its operations?

Globalization affords firms opportunities for rapid growth and significant value creation in a slow growth world. The process is complex and risky, however; globalization challenges firms' conventional notions about how to do business.

The growth of the global economy is a major trend in world business, a new landscape of rapid growth in world trade, investment, and financial transactions. Business opportunities are discovered and lost in the shifting sands of geopolitics and national suspicions and rivalries. A nationalistic backlash against globalization is gaining strength, but a countervailing communications revolution that is tying the world more closely together is likely to prove stronger. Businesses can safely pursue globalization, but the road will be more rocky than in the past decade. This is the shape of globalization as we enter the twenty-first century: a conflict between technology and trade, which are tying the world together, and geopolitics, which is pulling it apart.

twenty-first–century globalization

- Globalization in this century has been about "internationalization."

    Taking "existing" products to "new" markets; gaining access to high growth markets

    Exploiting scale, low-cost labor and supply, and exchange and interest rate advantages

- Twenty-first–century globalization will be about "value optimization."

    Focusing on market opportunities, not just cost advantages or core competence

    Configuring and animating networks; leveraging intangible assets; instilling global mindset

    Reinvesting the game (as through alliances, arbitrage, "not-invented-here") is good

- Strategy and execution become one in the three-step approach. Aristotle was wrong—strategy and execution are not separate. Firms must consider local and global tradeoffs simultaneously. It is essential that all managers adopt a global mindset.

Globalization at the firm level is usually construed in terms of the supply chain (finding cheap sources of supply) or the marketing function (finding new markets for a firm's products). But globalization also forces changes in the organization, affords greater opportunities for leveraging assets, and alters to whom firm leadership is responsible. (In the United States, for example, top executives are responsible to shareholders; in Europe, to a broader set of constituents including employees and communities; and in some third world nations, to a leadership elite or even ruling family).

A company becomes truly globalized by becoming localized abroad.

Firms need to base choices of location on value creation and what is necessary to achieve it. Value is most likely to be created today by increasing revenues, reducing costs, and leveraging assets. That even market leaders are failing to realize full potential value today is a function of myopia:

- business myopia (failure to see key opportunities or anticipate new challenges)
- organizational myopia (failure to recognize that the human resource element is failing to exploit opportunities afforded by technology)
- leadership myopia (failure to energize people in an organization and acquaint them with the changing expectations of today's environment)

The keys to success in the global economy of the twenty-first century are:

- an approach to business that forsakes centralization of strategy-making and business-planning in favor of a decentralized planning process;

- a different type of organization, the lattice; and

- a new type of corporate associate, one with a global mindset.

Strategic planning must be transformed from an event involving discrete sets of developers and implementers into a continuous process that involves all levels of the organization in the making and reviewing of certain kinds of decisions. The integration of strategy and execution is fundamental to the new business approach of *seeking* opportunity in the global economy, *shaping* the market, and *securing* the prize.

how one firm followed the
three-step approach

The early 1990s found the market for Sun Microsystems' powerful workstations being eroded from below by the rapidly increasing power of personal computers and from above by the significantly declining cost of mainframes. You read earlier how the 1994 Winter Olympics web site was born of a workstation shipped by Sun in response to a request from a group of network engineers in Oslo, Norway and that a copy displayed on Sun's own web site attracted legions of visitors.[1] Prompted by a customer in a foreign country to sally forth onto the Internet, Sun embarked, unknowingly at first, on a journey that eventually would dictate the adoption of a totally different strategic orientation in which the traditional process of strategic formulation apart from implementation played little or no part. Strategy evolved with execution as Sun began to recognize the formidable business potential of the Internet and, through it, a major opportunity in the global business environment.

What Sun subsequently did illuminates the three-step approach endorsed in this book as the key to success in the emerging global business environment.

- *Seeking.* Sun found in the Internet an opportunity to challenge competitors by offering its workstations as servers to customers in mid-sized firms.

- *Shaping.* Sun challenged Intel and Microsoft programming language, which enabled any computer to exploit the Internet's full potential. Sun's products went to market attended by considerable publicity and hype, enabling the company to attract alliance partners on a grand scale.

- *Securing.* Sun was positioned to profit handsomely when the Internet began to dissolve its competitors' hold on the market.

The formal process of analysis, strategy, and implementation could no longer work in Sun because recognition of the new business opportunity on the basis of which the company was redefined came from the rank and file, not from the executives or planners. The implementation sequence for exploiting this opportunity could not be explicitly plotted, but rather had to be developed in the daily turmoil of the marketplace.

Strategy and implementation are separated when staff and line are separated. Today's executives must be so involved in both that firms can no longer sustain their separation.

points to remember

e-leaders are responsible for:

- developing business opportunities via business arrays;
- reconfiguring the company into lattices;
- building a global mindset; and
- decentralizing planning via the three-stage approach.

The leadership challenge involves encouraging innovation without engendering fragmentation. Coherence, difficult to achieve in a turbulent environment, is the key to success. The object is to maximize the amount of innovation per unit of turbulence or minimize the amount of turbulence per unit of innovation. This is central to business success in the next century.

key principles of success include:

- strategy formulation in the flux of the market (via the three-step approach of seeking, shaping, and securing);
- strategic positioning at the business-unit level in business arrays;
- reconfiguration of companies into lattices; and
- cultivating a global mindset in all key personnel.

The new business e-Leader possesses a global mindset and e-commerce awareness. That is, he or she is aware of the global economy and the new technological possibilities and considers both in making decisions.

glossary

Business array: Firms, governmental units, not-for-profits, partnerships, and even individuals working in a common direction towards the creation of value. Competition is generally absent among the various elements; cooperative or transactional relationships such as buyer–supplier are sometimes explicit. A business array is larger than a firm, but smaller than an industry.

Business economics, the new: Characterized by increasing returns to scale from global reach and global interconnectivity.

Energized network: A high-performance global network that interconnects both electronically and physically in a complex quasi-formal structure; people motivated by considerable freedom of association and action.

Global mindset: A business characterized by an emphasis on searching the entire world for the best suppliers and customers; the most important driver of globalization.

Global network: Business elements of multiple companies connected via a formal structure that imposes order on the loose protocols of a network organization while simultaneously accommodating extensive customization and flexibility.

Global reach: Doing business wherever the best suppliers and customers are to be found; not only operating in many countries, but being at home all over the globe.

Globalization journey: The path a firm takes in the world marketplace.

Hyper-teams: Groups of experts assembled at a moment's notice via network linkages to work specific problems; analogous to Internet hyperlinks.

Interconnectivity: Communication linkages established via a host of mechanisms and media, including the Internet, intranets, and wireless telecommunications.

Lattice: A global network configured to exploit opportunities afforded by a business array.

Myopia, business: Failure to see key opportunities or to anticipate new challenges.

Myopia, leadership: Failure to energize people in an organization and acquaint them with the changing expectations of today's business environment.

Myopia, organizational: Failure to recognize that a firm's human resource element is failing to exploit opportunities afforded by technology.

Roles in an organizational lattice:

Initiator: Supplies strategic intent and vision, ensures the availability of the requisite resources for major activities, and usually designates the core management team.

Member: Performs a single value-adding activity; does not supply managers for the core team.

Player: Orchestrates array operations; manages resources for several linked activities.

Self-leadership: Authority to take initiative without prior approval of superiors; necessary to fully exploit the potential of interconnectivity.

endnotes

Chapter 1. The Unrealized Potential

1. Glenn Collins, "A Feeding Frenzy...," *The New York Times,* June 13, 1999, p. 37 ff.

Chapter 2. The Value-Creation Opportunity

1. United Nations data show that 151 nations, ranked from 23rd to 174th in terms of human development, experienced negative per-capita GDP growth from 1980–1992. United Nations, Human Development Report 1995, Oxford U.P., 1995, Table 20, pp. 194–195.

2. Arthur Schlesinger, Jr. has described the backlash as "the defensive reaction around the planet to relentless globalization—a reaction which takes the form of withdrawal from modernity." Arthur Schlesinger, Jr., "Has Democracy a Future?" *Foreign Affairs* 76, 5 (September–October 1997), p. 10.

3. See, for example, Patrick J. Buchanan, *The Great Betrayal: How American Sovereignty and Social Justice Are Being Sacrificed to the Gods of the Global Economy* (Boston: Little, Brown, 1998).

4. For some, globalism means that a dominant culture emerges in most or all countries. There are several ways in which this might proceed: through the synthesis of an "international" culture out of elements of many nations; through displacement of less advanced national cultures by a more advanced foreign one (seen either as cultural imperialism or progress depending on one's point of view); or through fusion of the same core foreign ideas into many existing domestic cultures to create hybrid but "converging" national cultures.

5. See, for example, S. Lael Brainard and David A. Riker, "Are U.S. Multinationals Exporting U.S. Jobs?" and "U.S. Multinationals and Competition from Low Wage Countries," *Journal of Economic Literature* Nos. J23 and F23 (Spring 1997).

6. Jeffrey Garten, *The Challenges of an Emerging World.*

7. Euro-Disney has had financial difficulties resulting not from a shortage of visitors, but from lower-than-expected expenditure levels and shorter-than-expected hotel stays by visitors.

8. Joe Rogaly, "No Spot . . . ," *Financial Times,* May 3, 1997, p. III.

9. Lionel Jospin, quoted in the *Financial Times,* June 7, 1997, p. 1.

10. Tony Judt, "The Social Question Redivivus," *Foreign Affairs* 76, 5 (September–October 1997), pp. 107 and 109.

Chapter 3. Identifying Business Arrays

1. *The American Heritage College Dictionary,* 3rd edition. Boston: Houghton-Mifflin, 1993.

2. John Hagel III and Arthur G. Armstrong, *Net Gain.* Boston: HBS Press, 1997, pp. 104–105.

3. It is important to note that all companies do not utilize the same core and enabling processes. Some may have unique competence, based on patents, which lets them use radically different processes. So a good consultant must ensure that the client's perception of core and enabling processes is reasonably consistent with those of its prospective partners or it may make positioning errors when choosing arrays to enter and activities to perform.

4. See Robert S. Kaplan and David P. Norton, *The Balanced Scorecard* (Boston: Harvard Business School Press, 1996) for a description of activity-based costing systems.

Chapter 4. Defining a Global lattice

1. Ian Steward, "Mathematical Recreations," *Scientific American* (July 1999), pp. 96–98.

Chapter 5. Configuring the Lattice

1. Interview with Professor Bower of Harvard Business School, 1994 (a videotape of the interview is on file in the school's audio-visual archives).

Chapter 7. Being Global

1. Peter Drucker, "The Global Economy and the Nation State," *Foreign Affairs* 76, 5 (September–October 1997), p. 168. Drucker uses a different terminology than we do, calling this kind of company transnational rather than global.

2. G.B. Friesen, News Corp., Andersen Consulting, 1996.

Chapter 9. Three Crucial Steps

1. Robert D. Austin, "Network Computing at Sun Microsystems," Harvard Business School case 9-198-007, 1998.

2. R.H. Coase, "The Nature of the Firm," pp. 33–55, in *The Firm, the Market, and the Law* (Chicago and London: The University of Chicago Press, 1988; paperback edition 1990). Quote taken from pp. 38–41. The original essay was published in *Economica,* n.s., 4 (November 1937).

3. Andrew Zajac, "Apple's Fallen Fruit," pp. D-1 and D-2, *San Francisco Examiner,* Sunday, February 15, 1998.

4. *Ibid.*

Chapter 10. Opportunity-Based Strategy: The Uniform Strategic Model

1. See, for example, Tom Copeland, et al., *McKinsey and Company, Inc., Valuation* (New York: John Wiley & Sons, 1994).

Chapter 12. Crisis in Corporate Leadership

1. Center for CEO Leadership, Atlanta.
2. Correspondence of Napoleon I, volume 32, pp. 182–183, quoted in J.F.C. Fuller, *Grant and Lee* (Bloomington: Indiana University Press, 1957; originally published 1932), p. 278.

Chapter 13. Avoiding Pitfalls

1. Andrew Davidson, "David Simon—Prototype of a Network-Managing CEO?" *Management Today,* July 1995, pp. 48–50.

Chapter 14. Embarking on the Three-Step Journey

1. Robert D. Austin, "Network Computing at Sun Microsystems" (Boston: Harvard Business School), No. 198-007, July 25, 1998, pp. 4–5.

index